Showcasing Mathematics for the Young Child

ACTIVITIES FOR THREE-, FOUR-, AND FIVE-YEAR-OLDS

Edited by
Juanita V. Copley

NATIONAL COUNCIL OF
TEACHERS OF MATHEMATICS

Copyright © 2004
The National Council of Teachers of Mathematics, Inc.
1906 Association Drive, Reston, VA 20191-1502
(703) 620-9840; (800) 235-7566; www.nctm.org
All rights reserved

Library of Congress Cataloging-in-Publication Data

Showcasing mathematics for the young child : activities for three-,
four-, and five-year-olds / edited by Juanita V. Copley.
     p. cm.
Includes bibliographical references.
  ISBN 0-87353-555-3 (pbk.)
  1. Mathematics--Study and teaching (Early childhood)--Activity
programs. I. Copley, Juanita V., 1951-
   QA135.6.S49 2004
   372.7--dc22

                                                2003023549

The National Council of Teachers of Mathematics is a public voice of
mathematics education, providing vision, leadership, and professional
development to support teachers in ensuring mathematics learning of the
highest quality for all students.

The publications of the National Council of Teachers of Mathematics
present a variety of viewpoints. The views expressed or implied in this
publication, unless otherwise noted, should not be interpreted as official
positions of the Council.

Printed in the United States of America

Contents

Contents

Contents

Acknowledgments

Editor

Juanita V. Copley, *University of Houston*

Editorial Panel

Ann Anderson, *University of British Columbia*
- Family Connection Activities

Beth Casey, *Boston College*
- Hanny the Honey Bear Discovers the World of Mathematics in the Big Zoo

Chuck Thompson, *University of Louisville*
- Young Children's Mathematical Thinking

Introduction

- Juanita V. Copley, *University of Houston*
- Chuck Thompson, *University of Louisville*
- Beth Casey, *Boston College*
- Ann Anderson, *University of British Columbia*
- Nicole Locher, *University of Houston*

Number and Operations

- Section Editor, Chuck Thompson, *University of Louisville*
- Activity Contributors
  - Chuck Thompson, *University of Louisville*
  - Juanita V. Copley, *University of Houston*
  - Ann Anderson, *University of British Columbia*
  - Beth Casey, *Boston College*
  - Brian Mowry, *Elementary Mathematics Specialist, Austin Independent School District, Austin, Texas*
  - Alice Klein and Prentice Starkey, *University of California at Berkley*

Geometry

- Section Editor, Juanita V. Copley, *University of Houston*

- Activity Contributors
  - Juanita V. Copley, *University of Houston*
  - Beth Casey, *Boston College*
  - Kristin Glass, Chancellor Elementary, *Alief Independent School District, Houston, Texas*
  - Julie Sarama, *University at Buffalo, State University of New York*
  - Douglas Clements, *University at Buffalo, State University of New York*
  - Ann S. Epstein, Director, *Early Childhood Division, High/Scope Educational Research Foundation*
  - Brian Mowry, Elementary Mathematics Specialist, *Austin Independent School District, Austin, Texas*
  - Christine Broadston, *ExxonMobil Math Path program of The Children's Museum of Houston, Houston, Texas*
  - Nicole Locher, *University of Houston*
  - Earl Snyder, Math Recovery, Chancellor Elementary, *Alief Independent School District, Houston, Texas*

Algebra

- Section Editor, Juanita V. Copley, *University of Houston*
- Activity Contributors
  - Juanita V. Copley, *University of Houston*
  - Beth Casey, *Boston College*
  - Jessica Mercer Young, *Boston College*
  - Ann Anderson, *University of British Columbia*
  - Emma Bruce, *Grand Prairie Independent School District, Grand Prairie, Texas*

Measurement

- Section Editor, Ann Anderson, *University of British Columbia*
- Activity Contributors
  - Juanita V. Copley, *University of Houston*
  - Beth Casey, *Boston College*

Acknowledgments

— Carole Greenes, *Boston University*
— Brian Mowry, Elementary Mathematics Specialist, *Austin Independent School District, Austin, Texas*
— Ann Anderson, *University of British Columbia*

Data Analysis

- Section Editor, Beth Casey, *Boston College*
- Activity Contributors
  — Irma Napoleon, *Boston College*
  — Ann Anderson, *University of British Columbia*
  — Juanita V. Copley, *University of Houston*
  — Beth Casey, *Boston College*
  — Brian Mowry, Elementary Mathematics Specialist, *Austin Independent School District, Austin, Texas*

Editor for Children with Special Needs

Rebecca Martinez, *University of Houston*

Mathematics Editor

Norene Lowery, *University of Houston*

Field Testers

(Space does not allow all the field testers to be named, but those listed below tested a significant number of the activities.)

- Cherry Alarid, *Bammel Elementary School, Spring Independent School District, Houston, Texas*
- Cathleen Auld, *Lamar Elementary School, Goose Creek Consolidated Independent School District, Baytown, Texas*
- Veronica Carlan, *University of Texas—Brownsville, Brownsville, Texas*
- Kellie Duffy, *Brazosport College Children's Center, Lake Jackson, Texas*
- Barbara James, *Bammel Elementary School, Spring Independent School District, Houston, Texas*
- Christine Broadston, *ExxonMobil Math Path program of The Children's Museum of Houston, Houston, Texas*

- Vanese Delahoussaye and students, *Child Development Department, Houston Community College*
- Javairya Khan, *Houston Community College*
- Nicole Locher, *University of Houston*
- Amparo Martinez, *Crockett Elementary School, Goose Creek Consolidated Independent School District, Baytown, Texas*
- Sarah Maxwell, *Dunn Elementary School, Arlington Independent School District, Arlington, Texas*
- Pamela Morse, *Houston Independent School District, Houston, Texas*
- Elizabeth Surratt, *Bammel Elementary School, Spring Independent School District, Houston, Texas*
- Sue Theall, *Neighborhood Centers, Inc.—Head Start, Houston, Texas*
- Karen Thomas, *Crockett Elementary School, Goose Creek Consolidated Independent School District, Baytown, Texas*
- Julie Whitis, *Starrett Elementary School, Arlington Independent School District, Grand Prairie, Texas*
- Tiffani Wood, *Saint Francis Episcopal Day School, Houston, Texas*

Chapter 1
Introduction

PURPOSE AND GOALS

Showcasing Mathematics for the Young Child: Activities for Three-, Four-, and Five-Year-Olds

is an activity book that highlights the mathematics concepts of young children. In our experiences with children as young as age three, we have found that they often play on their own using mathematical ideas and language. Further, we know that children can learn more mathematics than educational programs typically offer and that teachers often underestimate the potential of their young students to learn mathematics. We realize that early childhood educators incorporate mathematics in educational settings, but we have found that these educators often do not know how or when to facilitate early mathematics discovery. The purpose of this book is to illustrate activities that promote early mathematics development for children ages three to five and to "showcase" mathematics for the young child.

WHO IS THE AUDIENCE FOR THIS BOOK?

This book is written for all teachers of young children. Our definition of *teacher* includes parents, caregivers, private or public school teachers, and anyone else who is interested in the learning of young children.

WHY HAS THIS BOOK BEEN PUBLISHED NOW?

Recent legislation, such as the No Child Left Behind Act of 2001; a growing body of research about early learning (e.g., Shonkoff and Phillips [2000]); early mathematics curriculum projects funded by the National Science Foundation (Clements and Sarama [2003]; Ginsburg, Greenes, and Balfanz

> Study and the pursuit of truth and beauty is a sphere of activity in which we are permitted to remain children all our lives
>
> — *Albert Einstein*

[2003]; Klein and Starkey [2002]; and a resurgence of interest in the education of young children have all contributed to the importance of this work. In addition, the National Council Teachers of Mathematics (NCTM) included the prekindergarten level in its revised *Principles and Standards for School Mathematics* (2000). In conjunction with the National Association for the Education of the Young Child, NCTM has also published several volumes focusing on the young child and mathematics. *Showcasing Mathematics for the Young Child: Activities for Three-, Four-, and Five-Year-Olds* logically follows the edited volume of research (Copley 1999) and the more conceptual, practical book dedicated to children ages three to eight (Copley 2000). The activities in the current volume were written primarily for children ages three to five by teachers and researchers who are actively involved with these children and their learning.

HOW ARE THE ACTIVITIES ORGANIZED?

The thirty-five activities in this book are distributed into the following five content areas recommended by NCTM (2000):

- ◆ Number and Operations (chapter 2)
- ◆ Geometry (chapter 3)
- ◆ Algebra (chapter 4)
- ◆ Measurement (chapter 5)
- ◆ Data Analysis (chapter 6)

As recommended by NCTM, the number and geometry chapters contain the most activities (ten each), with measurement, algebra, and data analysis each containing half that number.

Each activity has the following components:

- ◆ Goals: Essential mathematical ideas, along with references to the NCTM expectations, as stated in *Principles and Standards for School Mathematics* (2000)

- ◆ Suggested contexts: Places or times in which the activities could be conducted, such as in specific learning centers, during transition or routine times, outside, in the community, on field trips, at home, as table activities, or on floor areas

- ◆ Recommended age ranges

- ◆ Materials

- ◆ Preparation suggestions

- ◆ Groupings: Recommendations for activity groupings, such as one adult and one child, two children together, small groups, whole group, or mixed groupings

- ◆ Description

- ◆ Suggestions for supporting learners

- ◆ Expectations

- ◆ Extensions

◆ Connections with (*a*) other mathematics, (*b*) the child's world and community, (*c*) other content areas, and (*d*) other centers

◆ Process standards addressed

In addition, many activities are highlighted by purpose or special content. Activities that include a literature source (1), a particular family focus (2), or adaptations for children with special needs (3) or activities that are extended over more than one session (4) are labeled on the activity pages to help the reader locate items of special interest.

Each content area is connected by a continuing story, "Hanny the Honey Bear Discovers the World of Mathematics in the Big Zoo." Placed at the beginning of each chapter, the experiences of Hanny are told through a variety of mathematical puzzles involving number and operations, geometry, patterning, measurement, and data analysis.

HOW SHOULD THE BOOK BE USED?

The foremost goal of this book is to foster the conceptual mathematical development of children. The grouping arrangements are flexible, the materials are relatively easy to obtain or adapt, and the contexts are offered as suggestions only. The activities in the book can be used in museums, early childhood centers, schools, or homes; on the playground; or as part of a field trip. Each of the activities has been tested in a variety of places with a diverse population of children. Teachers should use this book to help themselves teach mathematics, learn mathematics, and most important, "listen to children think!"

THE GROWTH OF MATHEMATICAL THINKING IN YOUNG CHILDREN

Research activity over the past forty years reveals that preschool-aged children develop a rich variety of mathematical concepts and skills, whether they attend a preschool or remain in a home environment (Ginsburg, Klein, and Starkey 1998; Sophian 1999; Starkey, 2003; Wynn 1999). This finding contradicts the prevailing opinion during the first half of the twentieth century, when it was believed that children's minds were empty until filled with mathematical knowledge by adults, especially teachers. We now know that children also learn by observing their environment, but they learn even more by interacting with it. They make sense of their environment, for example, by putting their playthings into groups and counting the number in each group. They compare one group of items with another to see which group "is more." They fill a larger container with sand by using a smaller container repeatedly and announce, "The big box holds three small jars of sand." In effect, they have measured the capacity of the bigger box by using the small jar as the unit of measurement. They find patterns in the clothing that they wear and declare that two cats and two dogs makes four pets altogether. They see a sign at a local gas station and say, "That's an oval just like the oval in my shape box at home."

At the beginning of each chapter in this book, we describe in detail the growth of mathematical thinking as it pertains to the content of that chapter. We present details about the mathematics learning that many children encounter at the ages of two through six. As you learn about the development of mathematical ideas in each of these areas, we recommend that you relate your new knowledge to the experiences you have had with young children. You may find that many of the ideas are familiar to you; indeed, you may even remember seeing similar behavior in your students.

NCTM CONTENT AND PROCESS STANDARDS

With the publication of *Principles and Standards for School Mathematics* (NCTM 2000), prekindergarten children were included in the *Standards* document for the first time; in fact, the first grade band was written for parents and educators of children from prekindergarten through second grade. The recommendations of the *Standards* were provided to assist parents and educators in giving children "a solid affective and cognitive foundation in mathematics" (NCTM 2000, p. 72).

The *Standards* document includes five content standards and five process standards. As mentioned previously, the content standards serve as the organizational strands for the activities in this book. Although many of the activities could fit in a variety of content areas, we have tried to locate them in one primary area and highlight connections with the others that apply. In each content area, the *Standards* document specifies a list of expectations for students in grades prekindergarten through second grade. The expectations for each of the content standards are discussed at the beginning of each chapter in a section called "The Big Picture." All the activities in this book include at least one of the expectations for the specific content standard. The complete list of expectations that are particularly appropriate for children in prekindergarten or kindergarten appears in appendix A.

The five process standards, which involve problem solving, reasoning, communicating, connecting, and representing, are applicable to any content area. Because of the general focus of these standards, the processes are discussed as they apply to specific content in the activities. We believe strongly that young children are capable of processing mathematics and concur with the assertion of the National Research Council that "[y]oung children…show a remarkable ability to formulate, represent, and solve simple mathematical problems and to reason and explain their mathematical activities. They are positively disposed to do and to understand mathematics when they first encounter it" (Kilpatrick, Swafford, and Findell 2001, p. 6). Along with the expectations for the content standards, the specific process standards are outlined in appendix A.

BEST PRACTICES IN MATHEMATICS FOR YOUNG CHILDREN: PROMOTING GOOD BEGINNINGS

In 2002, the National Association for the Education of Young Children (NAEYC) and NCTM issued a joint position statement with fifteen recommendations for early childhood educators to support the goal of ensuring "high-quality, challenging, and accessible mathematics education for three- to six-year-old children." (See appendix B for the entire document.)

> A major challenge of formal education is to build on the initial and often fragile understanding that children bring to school and to make it more reliable, flexible, and general.
>
> — *Adding It Up: Helping Children Learn Mathematics*

Because the first ten recommendations in this statement are directly related to the "best practices" proposed by NAEYC, they are listed below, followed by examples of the ways in which *Showcasing Mathematics for the Young Child* meets these recommendations.

RECOMMENDATIONS

To achieve high-quality mathematics education for 3- to 6-year-old children, teachers and other key professionals should—

1. Enhance children's natural interest in mathematics and their disposition to use it to make sense of their physical and social worlds.

Children often initiate activities that they enjoy or find particularly interesting. Many of the activities included in this book were created by young children and represent their natural interest in the world. Regardless of their genesis, all the activities in this book acknowledge the existing understanding and interests of young children.

2. Build on children's experience and knowledge, including their family, linguistic, cultural, and community backgrounds; their individual approaches to learning; and their informal knowledge.

Many, if not all, the activities in *Showcasing Mathematics for the Young Child* involve a variety of approaches to learning. The activities reflect the idea that young children learn through auditory, visual, and kinesthetic approaches. Further, numerous family connections are offered in each chapter, and most lessons include specific suggestions for adapting instruction to children with special needs or from diverse cultures or backgrounds.

3. Base mathematics curriculum and teaching practices on knowledge of young children's cognitive, linguistic, physical, and social-emotional development.

As we developed and field-tested each activity, we took into account the importance of children's physical, linguistic, and social-emotional development, along with their cognitive development. As a result, specific activities were included to emphasize physical development (Measuring March, Pom-Pom Toss, Block Tower), linguistic development (Creature Caves, Transformation), and social-emotional development (*Guess How Much I Love You,* Polling the Crowd, Time Capsule).

4. Use curriculum and teaching practices that strengthen children's problem-solving and reasoning processes as well as representing, communicating, and connecting mathematical ideas.

In each activity, one or more of the process skills are showcased. Connections are listed at the end of every lesson, extensions focus on additional problem-solving ideas, and questions provide reasoning opportunities. Oral, written, and pictorial representations are emphasized throughout the book, with many samples of children's work products to illustrate their mathematical thinking.

5. Ensure that the curriculum is coherent and compatible with known relationships and sequences of important mathematical ideas.

The lessons in this book include activities from programs developed through grants funded by the National Science Foundation. These programs emphasized the importance of "big ideas" and research-based curricula. This book is not a curriculum, but it suggests activities that could be used in a curriculum. Although the activities are described individually, they are grouped by content areas and arranged to connect with one another.

6. Provide for children's deep and sustained interaction with key mathematical ideas.

Young children often become deeply involved in exploring mathematical ideas, and this book is written to accommodate children who want to spend more time with certain activities. The extensions suggest additional activities for children who are especially interested in a particular concept. Many of the activities involve more than one session or task. Because children love to repeat favorite activities, repetition can also help sustain their interactions with important mathematical ideas.

7. Integrate mathematics with other activities and other activities with mathematics.

The activities in this book are not organized around themes; however, each activity has connections that suggest many possible links with other parts of the early childhood curriculum. These connections can be directly tied to the child's world, to other topics in mathematics, or to other content areas. Each chapter in this book continues the saga "Hanny the Honey Bear Discovers the World of Mathematics in the Big Zoo," inviting children to solve problems with the characters of the story. Additional activities that relate to the saga are provided for each of the mathematics content areas. Other connections, such as with art (Number Sculptures, Quilting with Paper, Triangle Blocks, Six-Pack Weavings), music (Writing Music, Pattern Count), and literature (*Benny's Pennies*, Making a Part-Whole Book, *Guess How Much I Love You*, *Mrs. McTats and Her Houseful of Cats*), are also included.

8. Provide ample time, materials, and teacher support for children to engage in play, a context in which they explore and manipulate mathematical ideas with keen interest.

Many of the activities are written to be part of centers or free play in classrooms. We believe in the importance of play for the young child and the potential for cognitive and social development in play situations. In addition, teachers' observations of young children at play are shared and discussed in each section.

9. Actively introduce mathematical concepts, methods, and language through a range of appropriate experiences and teaching strategies.

We believe that a range of teaching behaviors is appropriate in early childhood classrooms. Specific questions and examples of teaching strategies are included throughout each chapter. At times, we may recommend a direct teaching approach. In other instances, we may describe experiences and suggest questions or possible interventions. We may also present only the environment and materials, along with suggestions for general observations. Because the activities in this book are written to keep children actively involved with mathematics, the teaching strategies are varied, and some activities are written for whole groups; some, for small groups; and still others, as center activities or individual experiences.

10. Support children's learning by thoughtfully and continually assessing all children's mathematical knowledge, skills, and strategies.

Samples of children's work and responses are included for each lesson. Because the activities were field-tested with children of ages three, four, or five, the expectations listed should guide teaching and be helpful for assessment purposes.

THE IMPORTANCE OF OBSERVING AND LISTENING TO CHILDREN

The abilities to listen to and observe young children as they play with mathematical ideas are essential skills for teachers. We emphatically believe that teachers can learn a great deal about young children's beginning, informal knowledge by watching these children as they play and work. Thus, throughout this book, we describe young children's behaviors and their communications with their peers and teachers. These vignettes are printed in italics to help the reader identify them and discover the many interesting ideas of these "young thinkers."

Let us illustrate the importance of observing and listening to children with this example of young Harrison's block play, as described by his mother:

At age three, Harrison had difficulty connecting Lincoln Log pieces in his prekindergarten classroom. Some children could construct simple homes, but Harrison would often get discouraged with the construction and begin to play elsewhere. After admiring and watching his older cousins create large and complex houses, Harrison began playing with Lincoln Logs again and wanted to build big houses, "like Adam." Now, at age five, Harrison regularly plays with Lincoln Logs and not only has the coordination to construct simple houses but plans large, complex houses with windows, many rooms, porches, and doors. He even includes fences, garages, and other buildings. Harrison also adds train tracks; vegetation, such as trees and bushes; and animals and people to his creations. Often when Harrison finishes his structures, he engages in fantasy play, either replaying stories he has heard in books or creating stories of his own using trains, cars, and people.

One session with the Lincoln Logs was particularly interesting. Harrison talked to himself while playing, and his conversation was full of rich vocabulary demonstrating an understanding of numbers and problem solving. At one point he said, "I need a 'one,'" referring to the logs with only one notch. He was also heard saying, "No, I need two more ones" or "I need to take away this two and use a three, so it is stronger." This same day, I noticed Harrison eyeing his house, then looking around the floor at other toys. He picked up a green roof slat that is part of his log set, held it against the house, and said, "Three more." When I questioned him by asking, "Harrison, why did you use that green roof piece?" he responded, "Well, I couldn't tell how many more ones I needed on this side with my eyes, and this green piece is straight, so if I hold it across to the other side, I see how many are missing."

Who dares to teach must never cease to learn.

— *John Cotton Dana*

What did Harrison's mother learn from observing his work with Lincoln Logs? Many amazing things! First, she learned that Harrison developed complex structures given time and experiences with materials and other children. Second, she learned that young children naturally use numbers to communicate, and when they do, they often express number concepts in flexible ways. For example, Harrison used numbers both to label a block's notches and to describe a specific number of blocks. Third, his mother was pleasantly surprised at Harrison's description of his leveling procedure. Not only could he verbalize the process he used in detail, but he discovered a significant measurement procedure as well. What a good thinker! Through observing and listening, Harrison's mother gained a great deal of knowledge about her child that she can use to teach him even more.

STORYTELLING AND MATHEMATICS FOR YOUNG CHILDREN: "HANNY THE HONEY BEAR"

In *Showcasing Mathematics for the Young Child*, storytelling and mathematics are emphasized at the beginning of each chapter through the use of the saga "Hanny the Honey Bear," which involves children in solving mathematical problems for the characters in the story. We believe that storytelling is a powerful instrument that aids in introducing mathematical concepts and provides a method for practical application and understanding of these concepts for young children. One effective way to attach meaning to mathematics is to draw on children's love of fantasy and their imaginations by using adventure stories to teach mathematical ideas. (See, e.g., Casey, Paugh, and Ballard [2002] on block building and spatial relations; Casey, Goodrow, Schiro, and Anderson [2002] on shape attributes.) In addition, oral storytelling is a powerful medium to present mathematics because it appeals to children from a variety of cultures in which storytelling is an important part of the life of the community.

SUGGESTIONS FOR PRESENTING "HANNY THE HONEY BEAR"

A number of options are available for presenting the saga "Hanny the Honey Bear." The stories can be told as a daily activity over a week or two, perhaps connected with a theme on animals, or they can be used as introductions to new mathematical content areas as those are presented throughout the year. If you are new to the storytelling experience, you can use a combination of reading and speaking to tell the story to the children. Practice by rereading the story as it is written and telling it to yourself or others. Then combine the techniques of telling and reading with animation in your voice. As you become more comfortable with storytelling, you can relate the adventures using an outline for the important story and mathematical ideas and add your own details and embellishments.

Following the introduction to each chapter, animal illustrations identify the saga and accompanying activities of Hanny the Honey Bear. Characters are identified in boldface type before their speech in each story segment, and instructions to the teacher are interspersed throughout the dialog. The story section of each chapter may include initial mathematical activities interwoven into the story, and at the end of each story, Hanny must solve a mathematical problem with the children's help. This section leads directly into a mathematical activity and is followed by a brief story conclusion.

Hanny the Honey Bear Discovers the World of Mathematics in the Big Zoo: An Introduction

Teacher: I'm going to tell you about a special little animal who lives in a children's zoo. The children's zoo is a small building with baby animals inside of a bigger zoo. The special animal that lives there is Hanny the Honey Bear. Have you ever heard of a honey bear? Do you know what a honey bear looks like? What do you think they might look like?

Let's see what Hanny looks like [shows picture]. Hanny is not like an average honey bear. She can talk to animals, as well as tell stories to people, and she is going to tell us a story. Hanny is also special in another way because she loves to solve puzzles. For the zookeepers, Hanny's puzzle solving is an annoying habit because she uses this skill to escape from her cage. Because she can unlock any lock, her keepers finally put a lock attached to a keypad with numbers on her cage door. Guess what?! I'll bet Hanny can even figure out this number puzzle.

Hanny has a plan. Once she gets out of her cage, she has decided to go on an adventure and visit the big zoo. She is going to meet many new, wonderful animal friends, and so are you. But her adventure will be even more exciting because her new friends will introduce her to the world of mathematics, where new and challenging puzzles await her. As Hanny wanders through the big zoo, each animal will tell her a different mathematics problem, and she will have a great time solving them.

We're going to see if we can help Hanny figure out the solution to each of these puzzles and riddles as we follow along on her adventure. Here is Hanny to tell us her own story.

[The teacher brings out the Honey Bear stick puppet (see template in Appendix C) or other representation.]

Hanny the Honey Bear: Hello, children. I'm glad that you are going to come along with me on my adventure. I'm Hanny the Honey Bear, and I live inside the children's zoo house. Most honey bears live high up in trees in the rain forests of Central and South America. The children who visit often think I'm a bear because of my name, but I am not a bear. Animals like me are called honey bears because we love honey as much as big bears do and we look a little bit like tiny bears. We have big round eyes that let us see in the nighttime; soft, short, woolly brown fur; and teddy-bear ears. We have very long pink tongues so that we can get honey from a beehive or nectar from flowers. We are awake all night and sleep during the day. When we are awake, we swing by our long tails and feet through the branches of trees high up in the rain forest. Even though we look like little teddy bears with tails, you will be surprised to know that our closest relatives are actually raccoons, not bears.

I'd like to tell you about my life in the children's zoo. During the daytime, I often sleep. Sometimes I stay awake during the day, especially when my favorite zookeeper lets me play. As the children arrive, she introduces me to the visitors. When the children come close, she holds me by my tail, which I wrap around her hand. As the children stare at me, I stare curiously back at them. The children love to watch me lay on my back, delicately holding orange slices with my front paws while I greedily eat the fruit. My long tongue laps up the sticky juice from my paws and tummy when I'm done.

Sometimes during the day, my zookeeper has work to do at her desk, and she lets me stay with her, comfortably wrapped around her arm. Just like raccoons, I love puzzles and games, so I'm always figuring out ways to open the drawers or roll pencils off the desk. Sometimes my zookeeper gently scolds me, but then I wrap myself around her arm again and she goes back to work.

The problem for me is the nighttime. I am wide-awake all night long, and no one is at the zoo to play with me in my cage. I jump around with nothing at all to do. I am so-o-o bored. That's when I started trying to solve puzzles. My favorite puzzle is the lock on my cage door. My cage started out with a latch on the door. That was easy. All I had to do was reach through the cage bars and flip up the latch. Then I would push open the door and wander around the children's zoo house and discover all kinds of fun things to play with. When my favorite zookeeper discovered me in the morning, she would be mad at me for a while, then she would forgive me and let me play with her again.

The people who work in the children's zoo keep coming up with different ways to lock the cage door. They used a hook that snapped shut and a sliding lock that had to be pulled back. These puzzles were all lots of fun for me to solve. Finally, one day, my keeper snapped a lock on the door that was very funny looking. It had a pad with numbers on it. Oh dear! That one was too hard. I can't get out, and I have been bored every night since then. Tonight, I am determined to figure this puzzle out. Here's what the keypad on the lock looks like [see drawing at top of page 11]. Do you have any ideas on how to open it?

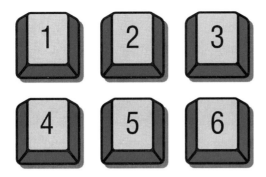

Here are the numbers that the zookeepers press when they unlock my cage.

[The teacher points with a finger to the key sequence that Hanny saw (1-2-3-6) and asks the children what numbers Hanny needs to press to solve the puzzle and get out of her cage.]

Hanny the Honey Bear: I don't know anything about numbers at all. How do you think I figured it out?

[The teacher asks the children how Hanny solved the puzzle without knowing anything about numbers. The children may need help identifying the spatial pattern of three buttons across the top, then one down on the right side of the pad.]

Hanny the Honey Bear: Here's what I did: I carefully watched how the zookeepers pressed the buttons on the keypad, and tonight, I have decided to try it out myself with my padded toes. Here I go.

Wow! It opened. I'm out of my cage. Great! You know, I have always wondered about the rest of the zoo because I have never been outside the children's zoo house. Here is my plan: I'm going to squeeze through an open window to visit the big zoo. I quickly scamper outside. I can sniff grass and trees and flowers for the first time. Can you smell that wonderful smell? My eyes sparkle as I gaze around this new world. I have arrived, and I am ready to start on my adventure visiting the amazing animals that live in the big zoo. Who knows? Maybe I will discover more puzzles to solve to keep me busy when I am alone in my cage at night. I am finally free to explore the zoo, and I thought it would be fun for you to explore with me. Would you like to come? What do you say?

Chapter 2
Number and Operations

THE BIG PICTURE

SELECTED EXPECTATIONS FROM *Principles and Standards for School Mathematics*

In prekindergarten through grade 2, all students should—

- count with understanding and recognize "how many" in sets of objects; ...

- develop understanding of the relative position and magnitude of whole numbers and of ordinal and cardinal numbers and their connections;

- develop a sense of whole numbers and represent and use them in flexible ways, including relating, composing, and decomposing numbers;

- connect number words and numerals to the quantities they represent, using various physical models and representations;

- understand and represent commonly used fractions, such as 1/4, 1/3, and 1/2;

- understand various meanings of addition and subtraction of whole numbers and the relationship between the two operations;

- understand the effects of adding and subtracting whole numbers;

- understand situations that entail multiplication and division, such as equal groupings of objects and sharing equally; ...

- use a variety of methods and tools to compute, including objects, mental computation, estimation, paper and pencil, and calculators. (NCTM 2000, p. 78)

YOUNG CHILDREN'S MATHEMATICAL THINKING ABOUT NUMBER AND OPERATIONS

Mathematical activity in preschools and kindergartens is often focused on number development. Children usually learn to count to 10, to write the numerals 1–10, to count sets of one to ten items, and to match one of the numerals 1–10 to a set having the same number of items. Those mathematical skills are important, but many other mathematical concepts and skills also warrant attention in today's world. This chapter addresses the following concepts and skills that are parts of the domain of mathematics called *number and operations:*

- ◆ Counting
- ◆ Comparing and ordering
- ◆ Equal partitioning
- ◆ Composing and decomposing
- ◆ Adding to and taking away
- ◆ Grouping and place value

Counting

Even before young children count, they are able to distinguish between a group of two items and a group of three items (Starkey, Spelke, and Gelman 1990). This ability to visualize small sets develops during the first eighteen months of life and later becomes more advanced. When children are four or five years old, many are able to identify patterned sets, such as those on dice, playing cards, or dominoes, without counting (Baroody and Wilkins 1999). For example, when shown the pattern below, many children automatically say, "three." Furthermore, this ability allows many children to see a group of five as one group of three and one group of two. This powerful knowledge enables children to take apart numbers mentally, work on them, and put them back together again in solving simple story problems.

Between the ages of two and five, children typically learn the sequence of number words from one through ten. This task is rather difficult because the words have no pattern; children must simply memorize them in order. At first, many children use a singsong approach, and "one, two, three" may sound like a single number name. At this stage, children do not know that the words they have said represent three different numbers and three different values. During the development of the number sequence from one to ten, children often leave out words unknowingly; for example, their count might be "one, two, three, seven, eight, ten." After much practice, feedback, and experience listening to others count, children learn the conventional sequence.

At about the same time or slightly later, children start counting objects, and this task is much more difficult than adults might imagine. Children must coordinate the act of reciting the number words in order with touching the objects they are counting one by one. Initially, children do the best job on this task when they have fewer than five items to count and the objects are arranged in a straight line. Some adults are surprised to discover that children must also learn that the last number spoken when counting a group of items tells the total number of items in the group. Understanding this concept is not automatic, but it is essential for all further work with numbers and such operations as addition and subtraction.

Young children are fascinated by large numbers and often learn to count to 30 by the time they are four or five years old. Their interest in large numbers motivates them to count to 100 at age five or six. They learn the counting-by-ones sequence for two-digit numbers by recognizing and using the patterns of number names, such as "twenty-two, twenty-three,…, twenty-nine," which is similar to "thirty-two, thirty-three,…, thirty-nine." Many children also learn to count by fives and by tens and recognize the similarity between "four, five, six" and "forty, fifty, sixty."

Comparing and Ordering

Young children can determine which of two groups of items "has more" by lining them up side by side and seeing which row is longer, but after age four, most children use counting instead. They form a mental list of the numbers 1 to 10 in order. They come to understand the idea that one number spoken after another number is greater than the first number. The question of "how many more" items are in one group than in another group is much more difficult, and young children need much practice with these types of problems to solve them effectively.

Equal Partitioning

Even three-year-olds can divide a group of items into equal groups if the beginning group consists of a small number of items. Four- and five-year-olds learn a "dealing out" strategy for larger groups of items. The equal-partitioning process is necessary for learning the concepts of division and fractional relationships.

Composing and Decomposing

Composing is the process of putting small groups of objects together, mentally or physically, to make a larger group; for example, a group of two and a group of three make a group of five. Decomposing is the process of mentally or physically breaking a group into two or more parts. Sometimes the ability to decompose is demonstrated by the child who "sees" a group of four and a group of one in a group of five items. This competence later becomes a powerful strategy for some children as they solve such a problem as $8 + 6$ by decomposing the 6 into 2 and 4, combining the 2 with the 8 to make 10, then adding the 4 to make 14 ($8 + 6 = 8 + 2 + 4 = 10 + 4 = 14$). Eventually, many children are able to find all partners that make up any given whole number that is 10 or less. For example, the partners that make 8 are 8 and 0, 7 and 1, 6 and 2, 5 and 3, and 4 and 4.

Adding to and Taking Away

Children as young as three already know that adding an item to a group increases the number of items in the group and that subtracting an item decreases the number of items in the group. They are able to solve simple story problems without formal instruction by re-creating the problem situation with chips, for example, then counting the resulting group of chips. Typically, they count to create an initial group, count to add or subtract a specified number of items, then recount the resulting group. As children develop their counting skills, they use them to solve problems more efficiently. They often "count on" from a number to solve a story problem involving $5 + 2$, for example, or "count back" to solve a problem involving $7 - 3$. These sophisticated counting strategies, combined with the ability to compose and decompose numbers, subsequently become powerful methods to solve word problems involving numbers to 10 and greater.

Grouping and Place Value

Grouping involves making sets of objects such that each set has the same number of objects. A child might, for example, make five groups of two

> Without formal instruction, young children can re-create a probllem situation with chips, then count the resulting number.

cubes for a total of ten cubes. Grouping in sets of ten is the basis for place value; for example, one group of ten chips and three more chips equals thirteen chips. Some kindergarten children can begin to learn about place value by making several groups of ten chips and some extra chips, counting the groups by ten (e.g., "ten, twenty, thirty"), then counting on the number of extra blocks (e.g., "thirty-one, thirty-two"). Almost all kindergarten children learn place value to the extent that they realize that the numbers 32 and 23 represent different quantities.

NUMBER AND OPERATION ACTIVITIES

The following table provides a brief description of each activity in the next sections.

NAME OF ACTIVITY	DESCRIPTION	PAGE
Hanny Learns to Count from the Prairie Dogs	Children count how many prairie dogs are in the burrows in several tunnels.	17
The Doughnut Game	Children use cereal pieces to represent number operations in an imaginary doughnut forest.	21
Number Sculptures	Children count and represent numbers using art materials. The representations are three-dimensional.	23
How Many Are Hiding?	Children guess the number of hidden objects, representing one part of a whole, by decomposing a whole into two parts.	26
Developing Pictures	Children visualize, copy, and make number quantities by adding to, and taking away from, groups.	28
The Sharing Game	Children partition a small set of cookies or bananas fairly.	31
Snaking Numerals	Children represent numerals using sock snakes or other bendable materials.	35
Tossing Pom-Poms and Making a Book	Children decompose and compose numbers by playing a game that involves the part-part-whole model. Then they create their own model and represent the number 6 for a page in a class book.	38
Food Fractions: Can You Cut It?	Children explore cutting food into equal parts, naming the portions, and sharing the food fairly.	42
Benny's Pennies	Children count with understanding as they "buy" items with five pennies.	46
A Calculator Game: Making Numerals	Children explore the calculator as they try to match single and multidigit numerals with the calculator display.	49

Hanny Learns to Count from the Prairie Dogs

STAGING THE SCENARIO

Make twenty paper-plate "mounds." Cut each paper plate as shown below, and tape them to form wide cone shapes. These mounds represent places for the prairie dogs to stand on, with the holes at the top providing entry into the tunnels.

Divide the room into four distinct areas, or tunnels. Place five mounds at random in one area of the room with large spaces between them. Place another five mounds at random in a second area, but space them closer together. Place four mounds in a third area in a line spread out as much as possible. Place six mounds in a fourth area in a line very close together. Bring out the honey bear stick puppet (see template in appendix C).

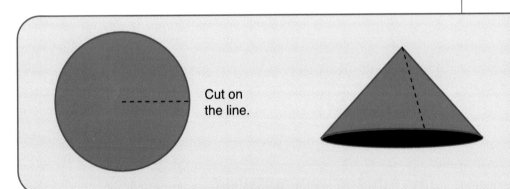

Cut on the line.

Fold the parts over each other and tape to form a cone-shaped "mound."

Hanny the Honey Bear: Are you ready for my first adventure? Gee, the outside world seems big and dark. Lucky for me, I can see with my night-time eyes. I wonder who is awake. Hmmm, do you see what I see? I see a big fenced-in area with lots of mounds sticking up in the air. Wait, someone is on top of a mound looking around. Are you ready to go over and meet our first zoo animal? All right, let's go. I am scampering up and over the fence.

"Hello, there. I'm Hanny the Honey Bear, but I'm really not a bear, so don't be afraid."

[Bring out the prairie dog stick puppet.]

Yippy the Prairie Dog: That's quite all right, partner. I'm on lookout, and you look fine, so come on over. My name is Yippy the Prairie Dog, but I'm no dog either, so I guess we're sort of even. Prairie dogs are really related to the squirrel family. Welcome to Prairie-Dog Town, partner. Prairie dogs are pretty friendly when you get to know us. When we're not in the zoo, we live out in the prairie country in the western United States.

Hanny the Honey Bear: Do you really live in a town? Where is it?

Yippy the Prairie Dog: Yes ma'am. Our town is underground because we live down in these holes in the ground. You can see where the holes are because of the mounds of dirt that are piled up on top. But underground, where you can't see them, are underground tunnels connecting all the mounds. When a prairie dog on guard sees something worrisome, it gives out a warning—"yip, yip, yip,"—bobs up and down once, then quick as a wink, pops into the hole.

Teacher: [to class] Can you try that? Pretend that you are the prairie dog on guard. Practice saying "yip, yip, yip," then pop up and down.

Yippy the Prairie Dog: That's the signal for all the prairie dogs to vamoose, ducking out and escaping through our many secret backdoors. Then we're safe and sound.

POSING THE PROBLEM FOR THE ACTIVITY

Hanny the Honey Bear: I am really curious about something. Can you tell me how many of you live in this prairie-dog town?

Yippy the Prairie Dog: That's for me to know and for you to figure out, partner. Yip, yip, yip! I can't tell you how many of us live in each tunnel of this prairie-dog town. That's a math puzzle that you are going to have to figure out. Look around our prairie-dog town and see if you can find out. I'm not saying this fact is true now, but what if just one prairie dog lived in each tunnel underneath each mound? How many prairie dogs do you think would be in this prairie-dog town?

Hanny the Honey Bear: Hmmm, this is a difficult problem for me because I never learned about numbers and I don't know how to count. [To the class] Do you think you could help me out?

CONDUCTING THE ACTIVITY

Goals: Count with understanding and recognize "how many" in sets of objects

Suggested Context: During a lesson

Recommended Age Range: 4–5 years

Materials: Two stick puppets, Hanny the Honey Bear and Yippy the Prairie Dog (templates for animal stick puppets are found in appendix C); paper-plate mounds; chart paper; unit cubes; drawing paper and crayons

Groupings: Whole class and small groups

Description

1. Ask the class to look around at the four areas, or "tunnels," in the room. Ask the children to predict which area has the largest number of prairie dogs. Remind them what Yippy the Prairie Dog said about the mounds. Record the class's predictions on chart paper.

2. Divide the class into four groups.

3. Assign a different area in the classroom to each group.

4. Give each group a stack of unit cubes to represent the prairie dogs. Pretend that all the prairie dogs are "on lookout," standing on a mound. Ask the groups to put one unit cube on each mound, then to return any unused cubes to you.

5. Give each group member a piece of paper and a crayon. Explain that each child will have to count how many mounds are in his or her group's area, then draw a picture showing where the mounds are.

6. Collect the children's recordings. Post them as close as possible to the area where the mounds are located.

7. Ask each group to report its findings. Discuss the pictures that the group members made. Collect and count the "prairie dog" unit cubes to check their answers.

8. After each group has reported, discuss how each area was different in spacing and in the number of prairie dogs.

9. Discuss how these numbers compare with the children's earlier predictions about which of the tunnels had more prairie dogs.

Expectations

◆ Some children may say that the tunnel area that looks the longest has the most prairie dogs.

◆ Some children will be able to count the correct number of prairie dogs just by looking at the tunnel areas; most, however, will need to demonstrate one-to-one correspondence to count the number of mounds.

◆ Some children's drawings will be surprisingly accurate and complete with numerals; others will make partial drawings; still others will have difficulty recording any representations.

Suggestions for Supporting Learners

◆ Make sure you draw attention to Hanny's question in the story that leads to the mathematics problem posed by Yippy, that is, "Can you tell me how many of you live in this prairie-dog town?"

◆ Point out that the paper plates represent the mounds over the tunnels and that you can't see the tunnels that are underneath. If children need help visualizing the tunnels, draw or find a picture illustrating an underground view of a prairie-dog village.

◆ In a group discussion after the activity, help the children realize the fact that the size of the tunnel does not correspond to the number of mounds.

Extensions

◆ Children can try to figure out how many prairie dogs are in the whole prairie-dog town.

◆ Have Yippy the Prairie Dog say, "I'm not saying it's true now, but what if two prairie dogs lived in each tunnel? How many prairie dogs might be living in the tunnels then?" Determine whether the children can count by twos.

◆ Later, the children can learn to count by fives. The teacher can judge how far to go, depending on the children's developmental levels.

◆ Have the children suggest other things that Hanny could count to keep herself busy at night.

Connections

◆ To the world of the child: Children enjoy counting activities and often count objects as part of the daily routine.

Process Standards Addressed: Children engage in problem solving and represent the tunnel area to help communicate their solutions to their peers.

CONCLUDING THE STORY

Bring out the honey-bear and prairie-dog stick puppets, and have them enact a culminating scenario similar to the following.

Hanny the Honey Bear: Thank you, girls and boys; you showed me how to count the number of prairie dogs in each of the tunnels. Now I will be able to count lots of things.

Yippy the Prairie Dog: Hey, partner. You are right on target. You did a great job counting the number of prairie dogs in my town. Yip, yip, yip! Hanny, what animal would you like to see next in the big zoo?

Hanny the Honey Bear: I have always wanted to see the very large animals that live in the zoo. The children's zoo has only little animals like me. Can you show me where these big animals live so that I can visit them?

Yippy the Prairie Dog: Hee, hee! The elephants should be big enough for you, darn tootin', and they're right over there. They should be awake, too, because they sleep for only two or three hours a night.

Hanny the Honey Bear: I'm off on another adventure to search for the big elephants and more math puzzles to solve.

The Doughnut Game

Goals: Understand the effects of adding and subtracting whole numbers; begin to compute using a variety of methods and tools, including objects, mental mathematics, estimation, paper and pencil, and calculators

Suggested Context: Mathematics center

Recommended Age Range: 3–5 years

Materials: A small plastic container, such as a margarine container, for each child and the teacher. Each container should be filled with ten to fifteen cereal pieces, such as small doughnut shapes. Each child and the teacher should also have a similar container that is empty.

Groupings: One adult with about five children

Description

1. Tell the children, "Today, we are going for a walk in a doughnut forest. Each of you has a container of doughnuts in front of you; that container is the doughnut forest. You also have an empty container into which you will put the doughnuts that you pick from the doughnut trees; we will call that container your basket. Along the way, we will get to eat some of the doughnuts we pick."

2. Then ask, "Is everybody ready to go to the doughnut forest to pick some doughnuts? What kinds of doughnuts do you think we will find today? What is your favorite kind?"

3. Lead the children through the forest by saying, "Here we go. I smell some chocolate-covered doughnuts. Let's each pick one from the forest and put it in the basket; now pick another one. How many doughnuts do you have in your basket?" Allow time for the children to count the two doughnuts in their baskets and explain how they obtained their answers.

4. Continue with the journey: "I think I see some glazed doughnuts. Let's each pick one and put it in the basket. How many doughnuts do you have in your basket now?" The children should now have three doughnuts. Be sure to observe how they get their answers. Do some of them count on? Do some automatically know that one more than two is three?

5. "I'm very hungry, are you? Let's each reach into our basket, get a doughnut, and eat it. How many doughnuts are left in your basket? How did you get your answer?" The children should now have two doughnuts in their baskets.

6. "Let's get some more doughnuts. I smell some lemon-filled doughnuts. Let's each pick two of them for our baskets. How many doughnuts do you have now?" The children should have four doughnuts.

7. Continue through the doughnut forest, having children pick doughnuts, put them into their baskets, and eat some of them. Conclude the activity by eating the doughnuts on the way home until the baskets are empty.

Expectations

◆ Children enjoy playing this game and often request it when given the opportunity to choose an activity. Children can also play this game in small groups and take turns being the teacher.

◆ Some children have well-developed number sense and will be able to give answers spontaneously. For example, some children will know that one more than two doughnuts is three doughnuts. Gather a group of these children, and use numbers in the story that are more challenging for them.

Suggestions for Supporting Learners

◆ For children who are having difficulty counting their doughnuts, have them remove the doughnuts from their baskets and line them up before counting.

◆ If the doughnuts are too small, use larger cereal pieces, even if they are of a different shape. Call them muffins, buns, or another appropriate name. Children can cup one hand and use it as a basket rather than use a container for a basket. Cereal pieces spread on a paper towel can also make the forest.

◆ For children who have dexterity or orthopedic problems, stabilize the containers on the table by using tape or self-cling strips. You may also need to use larger food items that will be easier for these children to pick up.

◆ Make sure that children who have hearing problems can always see your face as you lead them through the forest.

Extensions

◆ Gradually use greater numbers as you play this game with your students.

◆ Have children cover their baskets with one hand throughout the game, and challenge them to determine answers without peeking into their baskets. They may then look into the baskets to check their answers.

◆ Have sessions in which you focus on specific types of numbers or specific operations. For example, focus on adding or subtracting 2 repeatedly. This exercise can help children learn about skip counting and, perhaps, odd and even numbers. You might also focus on "undoing" addition by subtracting the same number of doughnuts that were just added. This exercise offers a preview of the inverse relationship between addition and subtraction that children will learn later. You can even ask the children to share their doughnuts with one or two pretend friends for a preview of division.

> Counting, adding, and subtracting are common in the lives of children. This activity uses common actions to develop important concepts about the operations of addition and subtraction.

◆ You may wish to state the addition, subtraction, multiplication, or division sentence that was solved each time and have the children repeat it. For example, when one doughnut is added to a basket that has two doughnuts, students would say, "Two doughnuts and one doughnut make three doughnuts."

Connections

◆ With the world of the child: Children love to shop, and this game is a little like shopping and eating what they have purchased even before they have returned home.

◆ With other mathematics: Patterns often arise when doing this activity, for example, counting by 2s or adding 1, then subtracting 1.

Process Standards Addressed: Children engage in *problem solving* in this activity as they find out how many doughnuts they have in their baskets. Further, they practice *communicating* their answers to their classmates.

Number Sculptures

Goals: Connect number words and numerals to the quantities they represent using various physical models and representations

Suggested Contexts: Art center or mathematics center

Recommended Age Range: 4–5 years

Materials: Piece of polystyrene foam for each child, perhaps about 2 inches by 3 inches; a variety of art scrap materials, such as straws, tongue depressors, ribbons, yarn, construction paper, golf tees, foam pieces, stickers, and foil; a number die; and pipe cleaners and glue. Some teachers use poster board instead of polystyrene for the base and colored cubes or pattern blocks to create a design or sculpture on the base.

Groupings: One adult and one child or one adult with several children

Description

1. Explain the activity by modeling a sculpture. First, roll the die.

2. Make a "sculpture" using the same number of items as the number rolled. For example, if a 3 is rolled, make a sculpture using three straws, three sticks, three red ribbons, three yellow flower stickers, and three blue triangles.

3. Have the children roll the die and make similar sculptures themselves.

4. Label the sculptures with children's names, and display them. Have other children try to guess what number was rolled on the die to make the sculpture.

5. Alternatively, have children describe their sculptures using position words, and have their peers try to identify the sculptures being described.

Expectations

◆ Children enjoy making the sculptures and may forget the number of items that they are supposed to be using. They may simply add lots of objects because they are pretty or particularly easy to place.

◆ Children may not use numerals or position words when they describe their sculptures. You may need to ask additional questions to help them make their descriptions more explicit.

◆ Some children may create symmetrical sculptures, whereas the work of others will be random. Observe children who are able to keep track of how many items they have counted for their sculptures and their specific procedures for doing so.

Suggestions for Supporting Learners

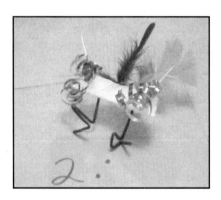

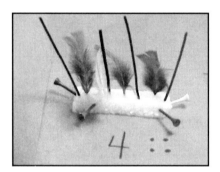

◆ For children who are having difficulty making sculptures with the correct number of items, ask them to choose their items before they put them on their sculptures. They should then ask their partners to tell how many they have of each item before they make their sculptures.

◆ For children who are having difficulty describing their sculptures, ask them questions using position, color, and number words, for example, "How many straws are on top of your sculpture? How many are under the foam piece? How many ribbons are blue? How many are curly?" You might also partially describe the sculpture, then ask the child to finish the description.

◆ For children who are having difficulty identifying the number represented by a particular sculpture, ask them to eliminate specific values represented on the die. Ask, "Could it be '1'? Why not? What about '6'? How did you know that the number wasn't '6' without even counting?"

◆ For children who have vision impairments, make your own die with numbers that stand out by gluing on objects that are flat on one side and rounded on the other, such as movable doll eyes, to represent the numbers.

◆ For children who have sensory deficits, the feel of polystyrene may be repulsive. Include other materials to make the number sculptures.

◆ For children who are easily distracted, providing too many materials may be overwhelming. Sometimes, using fewer materials may be better.

Extensions

◆ The sculptures can be made as part-part-whole models for numbers. For this extension, the foam piece is placed vertically on the table. Children again roll the die to get the number value. Then they put some of the items on one side of the foam piece and others on the other side. Children in the class may still try to guess the number represented by a particular sculpture, or the "artists" may describe their sculptures for others.

◆ The number die could be rolled each time for a different material. Then each kind of material could be used that number of times. Rather than roll a die at all, each item placed on the sculpture could be a different number, for example, one ribbon, two sticks, three stickers, four straws, five pipe cleaners, and six buttons.

Connections

◆ With the world of the child: Children need to see numerical values in the three-dimensional world, as well as in the typical two-dimensional world of school representations.

◆ With other mathematics: In algebra, children learn to make many models and representations of numerical values. The sculpture is just another way to represent a number. Further, the position words used to describe the children's creations relate to geometry and space.

◆ With other content areas: The creation of a sculpture is obviously related to art. Other art in the child's world can be described using numbers or position words.

Process Standards Addressed: Children *represent* number using art pieces to create a sculpture. They also *communicate* descriptions of their sculptures to their peers.

> Representation is a process standard. Children should learn to represent their understanding of numbers in many ways.

> All children should learn to recognize the number of dots on a die quickly, without actually counting them one by one.

How Many Are Hiding?

Goals: Count with understanding, and recognize "how many" in sets of objects; develop a sense of whole numbers, and represent and use them in flexible ways, including relating, composing, and decomposing numbers

Suggested Context: Mathematics center

Recommended Age Range: 3–5 years

Materials: A group of five to ten counters for each pair of children

Groupings: One adult and one child or two children together

Description

1. Complete this activity with one child while the others watch what you do, then have the children complete the activity in pairs. To begin, sit opposite the child.

2. Show the child the group of five counters that you have in your hand. Ask, "How many counters do I have?" Use fewer or more counters depending on the abilities of your students.

3. Put your hands behind your back or underneath the table or desk. Secretly put some of the five counters in one hand and the rest in the other hand. Close both hands.

4. Place your closed hands side by side in front of the child. Open one of your hands, revealing the number of counters that you have in that hand, for example, three.

5. Ask the child, "How many counters do you see?"

6. After the child answers, ask, "How many counters are hiding in my other hand?" Wait patiently for the child to respond. Some teachers wave a magic wand when the child "guesses" correctly. This action motivates some children to determine a strategy for finding the correct answer.

7. After the child responds, open your closed hand to reveal the hiding counters. Ask, "Were you correct?"

8. Have the child name the two parts and the whole, that is, "Three and two make five."

9. Repeat this activity with the same child, again using five counters but separating them into different sets, such as four and one. As you go through the following steps, ask the other children what the next step should be.

   a. Verify the total number of counters.
   b. Put your hands behind you, and separate the counters into two groups. Put some in one hand and the rest in the other.
   c. Place your closed hands in front of the other child.
   d. Open one hand, and ask for the number of counters visible.
   e. Have the child predict the number hiding in the other hand.
   f. Open the hiding hand to check the prediction and ask, "Were you correct?"
   g. Have the child name the two parts and the whole.

10. (Optional) Have two children demonstrate the activity using four or six counters as the others watch. Ask questions, and raise issues to clarify the steps listed in step 9.

11. Separate the children into pairs, and have them do the activity together. Have one child hide counters twice, then give the other child a turn to hide counters twice.

12. Have the children repeat the activity, this time, using a different number of counters. On the basis of your observations, suggest the number of counters for each pair to use.

Expectations

Older children might be able to "count on" from the number of visible counters to determine the number of counters hidden.

◆ This activity is sometimes used as an assessment of children's number development. You may want to assign children to groups on the basis of the results of these activities.

◆ These activities are intriguing for some children and not for others. Use these activities with children who are interested in them.

◆ Children may be reluctant to put zero counters in one hand, but you should encourage them to do so!

Suggestions for Supporting Learners

Provide extra counters for the child who is able to predict accurately. This child may use the extra counters to match the original number of counters revealed; then he or she can put out additional counters to make up the total and count the added counters to determine the number hidden. Younger children can use as few as three or four counters when they do this activity.

> Understanding part-whole relationships is an important aspect of number sense. When a child knows part-whole relationships, he or she can compose and decompose numbers in ways that are appropriate for the task at hand.

Extensions

◆ Use more than five counters.

◆ Have one child roll a die that has one to six dots on it. The other child should then say the number that is two or three more that the number of dots shown on the die.

◆ Keep tiles or counters in your pocket to play this game at any time.

Connections

◆ With the world of the child: Children love to play hiding games; after they learn this game, they may be eager to play it with their parents or older brothers and sisters.

◆ With other mathematics: Part-whole relationships become the foundation for many mental strategies that are used to solve basic addition and subtraction problems. Also, children who understand the structure of numbers and the relationships among them can work with them in many ways.

Process Standards Addressed: Children *solve* the problem "How many are hiding?" by *communicating* with others about their strategies.

Initially, children think that the ability to predict how many counters are hiding in the closed hand is magical! This perception motivates them to learn how to determine the number of hidden counters.

Developing Pictures

Goals: Count with understanding, and recognize "how many" in sets of objects; understand the effects of adding and subtracting whole numbers

Suggested Context: Mathematics center

Recommended Age Range: 3–5 years

Materials: A work mat (see preparation suggestions) for the teacher and each child, and a collection of about ten counters for each person to use

Preparation Suggestions: The work mat is made by taping a half sheet of colored paper on top of a full sheet of white paper. The colored

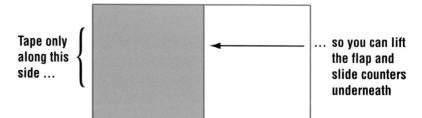

Tape only along this side ...

... so you can lift the flap and slide counters underneath

paper is taped along the left-hand side only to create a flap that can be raised and will allow the teacher or children to slide counters between the colored paper and the white paper. Laminating the paper before taping will extend the life of the mats.

Groupings: One adult with four to five children or one adult and one child

Description

Activity 1

1. Sit opposite the children, but make sure that everyone has the white part of the work mat oriented toward the same side of the room. For example, say, "Turn your work mats so that the white part is on the same side of the room as the window and the colored part is on the same side of the room as the door."

2. Tell the children, "Watch what I do." Place two counters on the white part of your mat, and lift your hand carefully to allow all children to see the counters. Do not help children determine the number of counters; they should create their own mental images of the group of counters. Then, gently lift the colored flap with your other hand and slide the two counters underneath it.

3. Tell the children, "Put counters on your mat to match what I have on my mat."

4. Allow time for individual children to place their counters, then say, "Let's lift up the flaps. Does your mat match mine? Are they the same? How do you know?"

5. Repeat with groups of up to five counters or, for some five-year-olds, up to ten counters. When you use four or five counters or more, display them in a patterned arrangement, such as those shown below.

Activity 2

1. Tell the children, "Watch what I do." Place two counters on the white part of your mat, making sure that the children can see the counters. Resist the temptation to count or help the children determine the number of counters placed on the mat. Then, gently lift the colored flap with your other hand and slide the two counters underneath it. The children do not place any counters on their mats at this point of the activity.

2. Say, "Keep watching; don't let me trick you." Place a new counter or, depending on the abilities of the children, more than one counter on the white side of your mat in plain view. Then carefully lift the colored flap *slightly* with your other hand and slide the new counter or counters underneath. Be sure that the children cannot see any of the original group of counters when you slide the new group underneath the flap.

Adding and subtracting are common in the lives of children. This activity uses common actions to develop mental concepts about adding and subtracting.

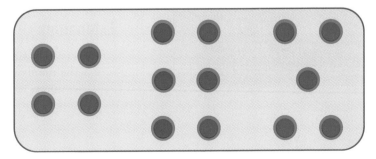

> You may be tempted to believe that the children are doing mental addition and subtraction when they successfully perform activities 2 or 3. However, some are simply repeating or copying the same actions that they see you do.

> Activities 1, 2, and 3 are sometimes used as assessments of children's number development. You may want to place children in groups on the basis of the results of these activities.

3. "Put counters on your mat so that it matches mine." Observe carefully to see how the children determine how many counters to place underneath their colored flaps altogether.

4. Provide time for individual children to complete the task, then ask, "Let's raise the flaps. Does your mat match mine? Are they the same? How do you know?" Ask the children to explain how they knew how many counters to put on their mats.

5. Repeat steps 1–4, adding one, two, or three counters to an original group of from one to five counters.

Activity 3

1. Repeat activity 2, but this time, *remove* one, two, or three counters from an original group of two to five counters that you have slid under the flap. Be sure that the children cannot see any of the counters under the flap except the ones that you remove.

Expectations

◆ In activity 1, some children will be able to create groups of two or three counters after watching you place the counters on the mat, then hide them, but they may not be able to create groups of four or more. This inability is considered to be normal development for children.

◆ Similarly, in activity 2, children are often able to increase a group by one or two items after watching you do so, but this ability diminishes as the number of items in the original group or the number of items added increases.

◆ These activities are intriguing for some children and not for others. Use these activities with children who are interested in them.

Suggestions for Supporting Learners

◆ For an exercise similar to activity 1, have children roll a homemade die with one to three dots on each side or one to six dots on each side and quickly say the number of dots on the top side. Alternatively, flash them one, two, or three fingers or up to five fingers; then hide your hand quickly, and have them show you how many fingers were raised.

◆ An activity that might help some children prepare for activity 2 is to say a number word from one to five at random and have a child say the next greater number. If you say, "three," the child would say, "four." Note, however, that some children can do activity 2 successfully but may not be able to do this "next number" activity.

Extensions

◆ For activities 2 and 3, have the children join you in saying the number phrases that match the actions, for example, "Two counters and one more counter make three counters" and "I had three counters, I took out one counter, and two counters were left."

Connections

◆ With the world of the child: Frequently, *Sesame Street* and other children's educational television programs show activities that involve identifying small groups of objects and matching them with the corresponding numerals. Also, children often see patterned sets on dominoes and playing cards.

◆ With other mathematics: Having a mental image of a set is necessary for a child to be able to "act" on a set mentally. That is, if a child has a mental image of the quantity three, such as three dots in a row, then the child can later mentally add one more dot and determine that the new total is four dots.

Process Standards Addressed: Children *represent* the numbers they visualize in many different ways in this activity. They must *reason* to predict the number under the mat after several operations occur.

Source. Dr. Arthur Baroody at the University of Illinois developed the original versions of these activities.

The Sharing Game

Goals: Understand situations that entail multiplication and division, such as equal groupings of objects and equal sharing; understand and represent commonly used fractions, such as 1/4, 1/3, and 1/2

Suggested Context: Small-group activity at a table in the classroom or at home

Recommended Age Range: 4–5 years

Materials: For each team of children, a pair of monkeys or other toy animals, miniature plastic bananas or other plastic fruit, paper cookie cutouts, two plates, one bowl; for the teacher, a pair of scissors

Preparation Suggestions: Create teams of two children each, and seat the teams at a table with you. Give each team a pair of toy monkeys, a plate for each monkey, and a bowl to hold the bananas or cookies to be shared between the monkeys.

Groupings: Small groups in the classroom or one adult and one child for the home activity

Description

1. Introduce the materials to the teams of children, and tell them that they are going to play a sharing game with two monkeys. Point out that each monkey has a plate for his or her food. Explain that this game is fair and that each monkey will get the same number of bananas to eat.

2. Tell the children that you will show them how to share the bananas so that each monkey gets the same number. Put four bananas in a bowl, and model the use of one-to-one correspondence to divide the bananas equally between the two monkeys. You can say, "Here is one banana for this monkey and one banana for that monkey. Here is another banana for this monkey and another banana for that monkey." Explain that when you share the bananas in this way, you give each monkey the same number of bananas to eat.

3. Ask the two children on each team to take turns playing the Sharing Game. The first child shares the set of objects while the other child checks the solution, then the second child shares while the first child does the checking.

4. Next present problems that involve sharing without a remainder; the following are examples:

    Problem 1. Divide a set of six bananas. Give the first child on each team a bowl containing six bananas. Tell the children that the two monkeys are hungry and want to share these bananas. Remind the children to be fair to each monkey. Then say, "Put the same number of bananas on each monkey's plate."

    Problem 2. Divide a set of eight bananas. Give the second child on each team a bowl containing eight bananas. Tell the children that the monkeys are hungry and want to share these bananas. Remind the children to be fair. Then say, "Give each monkey the same number of bananas."

5. Observe whether the children use the one-to-one-correspondence strategy to divide the bananas equally between the two monkeys. If any children do not use the one-to-one-correspondence strategy or make an error, provide extra support for learning. Then ask the second child on each team to check the solution by counting to see whether the same number of bananas is on each monkey's plate.

6. After checking, collect all the bananas from the children and play the Sharing Game again with the second child on each team.

7. Observe whether the children use the one-to-one-correspondence strategy to divide the set of bananas equally. Have the child who did not divide the bananas count the number on each plate to check the solution. Collect all the bananas at the end of the problem.

8. Next introduce problems that involve sharing with a remainder; the following are examples:

    Problem 3. Divide a set of seven cookies Give the first child on each team a bowl containing seven paper cookies. Tell the children that you are giving them some cookies for the monkeys to share. Remind the children to be fair to each monkey, and say, "Give each monkey the same number of cookies."

Observe whether children use the one-to-one correspondence strategy to divide objects equally in a sharing situation.

Problem 4. Divide a set of nine cookies. Give the second child on each team a bowl containing nine paper cookies. Tell the children that you are giving them some cookies for the monkeys to share. Remind the children to be fair to each monkey, and say, "Give each monkey the same number of cookies."

9. Observe what the children do with the remaining cookie. If children are not sure what to do with it, say, "That is a whole cookie. How can the monkeys share it?" If nobody suggests cutting it, you should ask whether it would be fair to cut the cookie. Then cut each team's remaining cookie in half with your scissors. Hold up a half cookie, and ask the children, "How much cookie is this?" If the children do not spontaneously answer that it is half a cookie, introduce the mathematical term *half*. You can say, "This is half a cookie" as you place a half cookie on each monkey's plate. Next hold up a whole cookie and ask the group, "How much cookie is this?" If no one uses the term *whole*, tell the children, "This is a whole cookie."

10. Ask the second child on each team to check the solution by counting the number of whole cookies, then the number of half cookies, on each monkey's plate.

11. After checking, collect all the cookies from the children and play the Sharing Game again with the second child on each team.

Expectations

♦ Some four-year-old children will have no difficulty using the one-to-one-correspondence strategy for problems 1 and 2 once you have modeled it. However, some children may place a few bananas on each plate without using this strategy.

♦ Other children may try to use the one-to-one strategy, but they may have difficulty and divide the set unequally.

♦ Some children may try to use counting instead of the one-to-one-correspondence strategy. If some children have counted, return the bananas to the bowl and say, "Now let's share the bananas another way without counting," In all these situations, you should help children use the one-to-one-correspondence strategy successfully.

♦ For problems 3 and 4, which involve sharing with a remainder, children may not know what to do with the remaining cookie, or they may offer solutions other than cutting it in half, such as setting it aside or giving it to one of the monkeys "who is really hungry!" Remind them to share all the cookies fairly, and ask how the monkeys can share the remaining cookie.

Suggestions for Supporting Learners

♦ If a child does not use the one-to-one-correspondence strategy or encounters difficulty in using it, provide scaffolding. Put the child's bananas back into the bowl, and model the strategy again by placing one banana on each monkey's plate. Then tell the child to share the rest of the bananas in the same way as you did. Provide additional help only if the child appears to need it.

◆ Use the words *half* and *whole* in different sharing contexts to help children learn these mathematical terms.

Extensions

◆ Make the activity more challenging for any children who correctly divide the sets of bananas and cookies into two equal subsets. Give the children larger sets of objects, and have them share the objects among more recipients. For example, a set of twelve objects can be divided among three or four monkeys. Extend the fraction portion of the activity by talking with children about other familiar objects, such as apples or crackers, to which the terms *whole* and *half* might be applied.

◆ Place the toys you have used for this activity, including many of the paper cookies, in the housekeeping or dramatics center. Invite children to continue sharing their food with everyone who is hungry!

◆ At home, sharing food is a common process. Ask children to help their parents "be fair."

◆ Develop a restaurant or cookie-store center. Provide many paper models of food that can be "shared fairly" with the customers in the restaurant or store.

Connections

◆ With the world of the child: Children are familiar with the term *sharing*, and at this age, they have developed their own concept of fairness. This activity provides an opportunity to discuss fairness from a mathematical perspective. Also, children will participate in many play experiences that involve sharing fairly.

Process Standards Addressed: Children engage in problem *solving* to share cookies and bananas fairly. They also must *reason* to decide whether one of their actions is fair.

Source: This activity is adapted from *Pre-K Mathematics Curriculum,* by Prentice Starkey and Alice Klein (Glenview, Ill.: Scott Foresman, 2002) (ISBN: 0-328-02298-5). Evaluation research on this curriculum was supported by the U.S. Department of Education/OERI Grant R307F60024.

Snaking Numerals

Goals: Develop a sense of whole numbers, and represent and use them in flexible ways; connect number words and numerals with the quantities they represent by using various physical models and representations

Suggested Contexts: At home or in the mathematics center

Recommended Age Range: 3–5 years

Materials: Clean, discarded adult socks and plastic shopping bags or other stuffing material; felt or other recyclable objects or materials for eyes and tongue; needle and thread for sewing; and magnetic numerals or a poster or book that illustrates numerals. Thick yarn or modeling clay may also be used as a substitute for the sock snake.

Groupings: One adult and one child or one adult and a small group of children.

Description

> The toddler excitedly squealed, "It's a '2'! It's a '2'! I made a '2'!" Mom came running to find her daughter's sock snake twisted into a curvy shape similar to the numeral 2. So began a game between mother and daughter: Mom might curl the sock snake into some numeral on the bed to be discovered the next morning, or the daughter might purposely or accidentally curl the snake into a numeral and await her mother's gaze and exclamations.

Preparation Suggestions

Follow the directions below to make a sock snake at home or at school. Involve children in the creation of their own sock snakes as much as possible. Try to make at least two or three snakes.

1. Collect at least three clean, discarded adult socks, sewing needle and thread, materials for eyes and tongue, and a number of plastic shopping bags for stuffing.

2. Stuff two socks to form the back and front of the snake.

3. Cut off the toe of the third sock so that it can be attached to the others to form the middle of the snake.

4. Using a blunt tapestry needle, the child may help an adult sew one end of the middle sock to the open end of a stuffed front sock, either edge to edge or by overlapping the edges.

5. Stuff the middle section quite full, then sew on the remaining stuffed sock. You should now have a long closed tube that is bendable.

6. Glue or sew on felt or button eyes on one end of the tube to form a face.

7. Make a long red tongue out of felt, paper, or ribbon, and sew or glue it to the head. For a mouthlike effect, push into the end of the sock to form a small pocket, place one end of a tongue in the pocket, and sew the two new edges to form a closed mouth with a protruding tongue.

8. Let children play with the completed snakes, slithering them around a tabletop or on the floor to explore how the snakes bend and curl. If sock snakes are school "pets," children can take them home for an overnight visit, accompanied by the following note:

   > Hello, my name is [snake's name]. You and your child can have fun making numbers with me. When you curl me into a 6 or a 2, say what number I look like, 6 or 2. Ask your child to curl me into other numbers, such as 7 or 1. You or your child can curl me into any number and ask what number I am. You might want to play this game with me a few times, then let me take a rest, instead of doing a lot of numbers one after the other, because I tire easily. I'm looking forward to playing numbers with you.

9. In school or at home, the sock snake may stay in a place where other forms of numerals are stored. Provide as many examples of numerals as appropriate, such as foam, cardboard, or magnetic numerals; counting books, books with numerals in the illustrations, or books that have clearly visible page numbers; posters of numerals alone or numerals on objects; and toys or other objects, such as plastic telephones, child-size calculators, and clocks that have colorful numerals.

10. Ask children to use two or more snakes to show a favorite numeral. After showing several numerals, ask each child to choose one "snake numeral" to record. If a camera is available, an adult can assist children in taking photographs of their snake numerals. An adult can also help a child slip a large sheet of paper under the snake numeral to help the child trace its outline. Encourage children to paint or color the numeral outline to resemble the sock-snake numeral created.

Although this activity focuses primarily on the numeral representation, a numeral should be associated as often as possible with the quantity it represents.

Expectations

Most children need help identifying and naming a numeral in isolation. Some children require more assistance than others in curling a snake into a numeral-like shape.

◆ Some children may see numerals as a continuous formation, whereas others see them as a formation of several distinct lines. Consequently, when building a 5, some children may form one snake into a fluid, misshapen S, whereas others may position one snake horizontally at the top, another vertically, and a third curled into a backward C. Some children may even form the C part of the 5 by placing three more snakes in a horizontal-vertical-horizontal line pattern. Having the opportunity to try both ways is beneficial.

◆ Teachers should expect to see typical developmental signposts, such as reversals or confusion of 6s and 9s. Modeling the correct formation is appropriate, but you do not need to impose it on the child. Of course, because these constructions are usually formed on a large open area, such as a carpeted floor or a table, and participants can walk around the snakes, the orientation of the numeral is of less concern than when one assumes the left-to-right reading pattern for print.

Suggestions for Supporting Learners

Permit and encourage a child to watch and assist you in making snake numerals. Provide opportunities for both observing and copying your actions. As you form the numerals, talk about the features of the numeral that help you decide how to curl the snake.

◆ For children who hesitate or are perplexed, suggest such numerals as 1 or 7 to begin. Supplying construction-paper templates of the numerals onto which a snake may slither proves helpful for some children.

◆ For children who have visual difficulties, allow them to squeeze the sock snake to feel the numeral form.

◆ If children do not have sensory impairments, let them feel the softness of the sock and hear the crackling of the plastic bags inside.

◆ If children are having difficulty making the sock-snake numbers, make large numeral cards. Glue rice or sand over the numerals, and let dry. Children can then touch and trace the resulting numerals. Sand trays or gel bags can also be used for tracing numerals.

Extensions

◆ Pose open-ended challenges for the children to think about and create with their snakes, for example, "Which of the numerals is like the letter S? Which numeral cannot be made with only one snake? Which numeral looks exactly like another numeral when turned upside down?"

◆ Ask children to make a numeral using a corresponding number of snakes, for example, "Make '5' using five snakes." Ask children to create a multidigit numeral from their environment, such as a house number, a page number, or a telephone number, using sock snakes. Ask, "How many digits are in the number? How many snakes did you need?" Keep in mind that 27, for example, is a two-digit number, but two, four, or more snakes could be used to form the numeral.

◆ Make a class or home collection of decorative numerals found in magazines, on clothes, in pictures, or in newspapers. Encourage parents to locate numerals with their children as they drive in a car, walk to school, or wait for the daycare bus. Take pictures of numerals you see.

Connections

◆ With the world of the child: Numerals abound in a child's environment and often come in varied, decorative forms. Numbers on houses, on appliances, on playing cards, in board games, in picture and coloring books, and so on, are written in different ways and differ in shape and size. Some everyday objects look like numerals, such as a baby's teething ring that looks like the numeral 8.

◆ With other content areas: Recycling and reusing socks and plastic bags to create a toy can lead to an informal environmental lesson. Written and oral language and reading are connected with this activity through the note sent home with each child and could easily be extended into creative writing about "The Adventures of Socksnake in Numberland."

Process Standards Addressed: Children *represent* numerals in a variety of forms and *communicate* about their representations.

Tossing Pom-Poms and Making a Book

Goals: Develop a sense of whole numbers, and represent and use them in flexible ways, including relating, composing, and decomposing numbers

Suggested Context: Mathematics center

Recommended Age Range: 3–5 years for Tossing Pom-Poms; 5 years for Making a Book

Materials: Colored pom-poms used for crafts; a meter of yarn tied in a loop or a hula hoop; recording paper and crayons or markers; *Five Creatures* (Jenkins 2001) or any similar book that shows multiple ways of decomposing a set into subsets; plastic rings from beverage six-packs; and a stapler

Groupings: One adult and one child, two children together, or one adult and several children

Description

Activity 1: Tossing Pom-Poms

1. Have each child select the number of pom-poms that matches her or his age, that is, three pom-poms if the child is three, four if the child is four, and so on.

2. Place the yarn on the floor, and stretch it out to form a large loop.

3. Tell each child to walk "like a tightrope walker" and take the same number of steps away from the loop as his or her age, that is, three steps if the child is three, four steps if the child is four, and so on.

4. Have each child turn around and toss the pom-poms one at a time into the loop.

5. Have the child count the number of pom-poms inside and outside the loop.

6. Ask the child to record the results. Children can draw and color a picture to show the pom-poms inside and outside the loop (see sample dawing in the sidebar), or they can use other representations to show their results. They might also write numerals to show how many pom-poms are inside and outside.

7. Children should try the activity at least three times if they are three, four times if they are four, and so on, or they may do the activity as many times as they like!

Activity 2: Making a Book

1. Read *Five Creatures* (Jenkins 2001) to a group of five children. Each page describes a clever scenario involving decomposing the number 5 into two or more parts. One example from the text is "Five creatures live in our house ..." (p. 1). "Three with orange hair, and two with gray" (p. 4).Challenge the children to figure out who is who by looking at the book's illustrations. For this example, the three with orange hair are the mom, the daughter, and one cat; the two with gray hair are the dad and the other cat. Children will love this intriguing book!

2. Ask the children to name the parts of 5 described in each scenario, for example, three people and two cats or one person who likes beets and four who do not like beets.

3. Ask the children how each page is like the activity Pom-Pom Toss, and make the connection that both show ways of separating a group of items into parts.

4. Tell the children that they are going to make a book about 6 and the different ways that 6 can be separated into parts.

5. Give each child a sheet of paper, markers, a set of plastic rings from a beverage six-pack, and at least twelve counters, six each of two different colors. Ask each child to make a page for the book. Start by having the children put six chips in their plastic rings, one in each ring, as shown below. Initially, have them use some chips of each color. Have

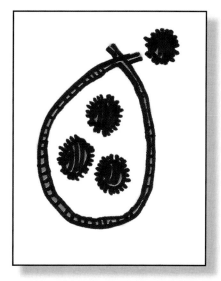

This activity leads nicely into an introduction of the part-part-whole model. The whole is the total number of pom-poms tossed for each turn, and the parts are the pom-poms inside and outside the circle. Thus, the two parts sum to make the whole.

each child decide what she or he wants the chips to represent. They could be creatures described in *Five Creatures* or any other items. For example, a child might want to let the red chips be squirrels and the yellow chips be birds. Then have the child draw the four squirrels and two birds on the sheet of paper.

6. As the children finish their pages, have them verbalize the part-whole relationships. For example, a child might say, "I drew four squirrels and two birds; that is six animals in all."

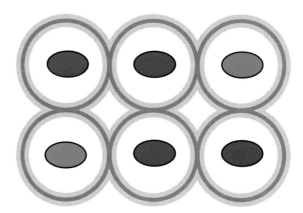

> The various part-whole relationships for 6 are sometimes known as the number family for 6.

7. Have each child look to see other ways of making 6 that other students are drawing, and make a new drawing showing one of these other combinations if possible. Note that drawing two cats and four dogs is a different way of making 6 than drawing four cats and two dogs.

8. When the children are finished, lay out all the pages and ask the children if all the ways of making 6 are shown. Have them verbalize the part-whole relationship on each page, for example, "Four and two make six." If not all part-whole relationships for 6 have been shown, ask children which ways have not been shown and lead them in finding and making the missing combinations.

9. Stack all the pages together in order, and staple them to make a book. A possible title would be *Our Book about 6*.

Expectations

◆ Children love the activity Tossing Pom-Poms. They are challenged to see how many pom-poms they can get inside the loop each time and will try the game over and over. Children who are four soon learn that three pom-poms inside the loop means that only one is outside; children who are five discover that they can get three pom-poms inside the loop and two outside quite easily.

◆ Children will seldom if ever record a score of zero inside and all the remaining pom-poms outside, but they will often record a score representing all the pom-poms inside and zero outside. Either situation presents a natural opportunity to introduce the concept of 0.

◆ In making the book, some children will quickly think of a variety of part-whole relationships for 6, but others will have difficulty finding even one. You may want to allow those children who think quickly to make their own books for 6 or a number that is greater than 6; challenge these students to find all possible part-whole combinations for the numbers they have been assigned.

◆ Because the drawing skills of young children are sometimes limited, you may have difficulty determining what the children have drawn on their book pages and what the two parts of 6 are. Having children use one color to draw one of their parts of 6 and a different color to draw the other part may be helpful.

Suggestions for Supporting Learners

◆ For children who have difficulty selecting a specific number of pom-poms, count out the number using finger representations of their ages. Most children know how old they are by showing their fingers. Ask them to place their fingers down on the desk or table and place one pom-pom next to each finger.

◆ For children who have difficulty tossing the pom-poms and getting any inside the loop, ask them to take "baby steps" away from the loop or hold their hands over the loop vertically at eye level.

◆ For children who have difficulty counting and recording the results of Tossing Pom-Poms, assign a partner who can record while the first child counts, or vice versa. As each pom-pom is picked up, the recording should be drawn.

◆ Ask those who can count and record easily to group all their recording sheets that are alike, such as all sheets that show three pom-poms inside and one outside, in one pile. These students can also play the game using their ages plus one or two, recording and sorting the results for each number.

Extensions

◆ Ask children of the same age to meet in small groups with the teacher and discuss the pom-pom results. All the recording sheets can be grouped to place all similar results together. For example, for a group of five-year-olds, all the results that show zero pom-poms inside and five outside can be in one group; one inside and four outside can be in another group; and so on. Then the results can be graphed to help the children notice patterns. A partial graph for this task might look like this:

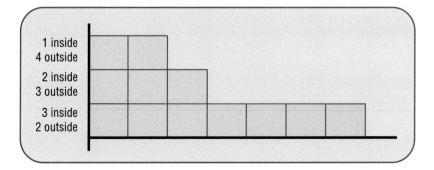

◆ Ask children to hold up six fingers, and describe their arrangements. Some children will hold up five and one; others will show three and three or four and two.

Connections

◆ With the world of the child: Children naturally love to talk about their ages and to play games that involve their ages plus one or two. They also enjoy physical games and may play Tossing Pom-Poms outside using small game markers and loops drawn on the sidewalk. Children often sort their toys, dolls, or trading cards into sets. Each of these activities is an example of discovering a part-whole relationship.

◆ With other mathematics: The extension activity that involves grouping and graphing the results of the game is an example of data analysis. This activity also promotes understanding of fact families, which is essential for building number sense and preparing to learn whole-number operations.

◆ With other content areas: Tossing Pom-Poms helps young children practice motor skills.

Process Standards Addressed: Children *reason* about different ways to make parts of 6 and other possible arrangements for the number 6. Their *representations* of their game results and the part-part-whole book offer many different ways of "seeing" 6.

Source: *Five Creatures,* by Emily Jenkins (New York: Farrar, Straus and Giroux, 2001).

Food Fractions: Can You Cut It?

Goals: Understand and represent commonly used fractions, such as 1/4, 1/3, and 1/2.

Suggested Contexts: At home, during snack time, as a table activity

Recommended Age Range: 3–5 years

Materials: Homemade or commercial modeling clay; bread or cookie dough; food, such as cheese slices, apples, sandwiches, or toast; plastic knife; wooden stir stick; plastic pizza cutter; small rolling pins or smooth cylinders; paper pieces to represent food

Groupings: One adult and one child or a small group of children

Description

"You made a pizza with modeling clay. Let's cut it so that all four of us get a piece. First we need to cut it in half." "Right down the middle" says the four-year-old daughter as she makes a vertical cut with her plastic knife. "Now we need to cut it in half again," encourages her mother. "This way?" asks the daughter, indicating a vertical cut down the middle of one of the semicircles. "Will each piece be the same? Let's cut these pieces in half this other way and see what happens," says the mother. The child cuts horizontally through the middle of each semicircle. "Four equal pieces make the whole thing. Would you like one-fourth of your pizza?" asks the mother.

1. Prepare snacks or lunches together. Allow a child to cut whole food items, such as sandwiches, cheese slices, toasted bread, or large cookies, into equal parts. Vary both the food to be cut and the ways in which the child may cut it. Be sure to compare the fairness of the pieces the child creates by asking, "Are the pieces of equal [or the same] size?" Model a variety of ways for cutting food into equal portions. When cutting toast in half, sometimes use a diagonal cut; at other times, use a horizontal cut across the middle. Use fraction language to describe the portions. Speak of "one-fourth" of the apple, as well as "one of the four" pieces.

2. Organize a snack challenge. To make a sandwich tray for the class to share, for instance, challenge each child to cut a whole sandwich into four equal rectangles, triangles, or squares. Remember that even un-expected shapes are edible fractions if they are equal portions of the whole. As the children place their sandwich pieces on the tray, use fraction names to describe the pieces in terms of the whole sandwich, for example, "You are placing two-fourths of your sandwich at a time, I see." If a child wonders about whether a triangle "one-fourth" is the same as a square "one-fourth," informally discuss ways to find out.

3. Pose a similar challenge as a table activity. Cut orange cardboard into square replicas of cheese slices, then cut these pieces into halves or quarters in various ways, that is, into triangles, squares, and rectangles. On at least one portion, write "1/4, one-fourth" or "1/2, one-half" and place the cut pieces of cardboard cheese squares into individual bags. Keep some of the cardboard cheese slices whole. Cut brown cardboard into square and rectangular replicas of crackers so that the cheese portions, that is, the fourths or halves, fit on top of them reasonably well. Place the crackers on a paper plate or tray. Have the children cover the crackers with cheese and, when all the crackers are covered, pretend to have a snack. This same procedure can be followed using modeling clay. Later, the paper or clay food can be added to the house or restaurant center.

When they try to separate a region into more than two equal parts, young children usually repeat the same cutting action.

Expectations

◆ Many children separate "breakable" food in halves or fourths informally when trying to share with friends or siblings, but the results are not always equal portions. Such initial experimentation supports further development.

◆ Children of ages three to five typically make vertical and horizontal cuts. Initially, children tend to use only one type of cut and repeat it as many times as needed to get the number of pieces desired. This strategy usually proves to be more successful in creating equal portions when a square or rectangle is being cut and less so when a circle is used. The need to combine horizontal and vertical cuts to create fourths may occur spontaneously for some children, but some will need explicit modeling of such a strategy.

◆ Conventional fraction language beyond *one-half* is not known to many children of this age. They need to hear and use other examples of fraction language, such as *one-fourth* or *three-fourths*, in meaningful contexts.

Suggestions for Supporting Learners

◆ Point out what you notice about how things are cut, and ask the children what they notice. For example, a combination of horizontal and vertical cuts is used to create individual servings of lasagna or cookie bars. Pointing this fact out to children provides background experience on which they can draw when they experiment with their own cutting.

◆ Allow children to assist in cutting a variety of materials into fractions for different reasons. Also allow and encourage children to do their own cuts and to compare the pieces that result. Allow for free play and experimentation. Try to use a variety of shapes to be partitioned.

◆ For some children, concentrating on halves or quarters is sufficient, whereas others are ready for thirds. Folding napkins in half, cutting cookies in half, and so on are everyday experiences from which children benefit. Having a tea party with two or three favorite toys is a common play context that readily suggests cutting real food items or clay models into three or four equal pieces.

◆ Connect the fraction terms *one-half, one-quarter,* or *two-quarters* with the portions of food they represent. For example, when naming *one-fourth*, hold one of the four pieces of a sandwich in your hand and refer to it directly as one-fourth of the sandwich. When talking about how many parts make the whole, have the child put the pieces together to form the original whole. When examining equal portions, have children compare the parts as directly as possible by overlaying the pieces.

◆ Radial cuts are difficult to execute, yet we usually use these cuts on circular items. When cutting pies, cakes, pizza, and so on, we usually cut from a center point toward the edge. Try to involve children as observers and participants in cutting circular objects.

Extensions

◆ Repeat similar activities, and incorporate less common fractions, such as thirds. Using circles to create thirds adds to the difficulty of this activity, and using rectangles lessens it for most children.

◆ Fold or cut linear items, such as rope, licorice, or ribbon, into halves, thirds, and fourths. Some children find such tasks easier than cutting rectangular or circular regions.

◆ Provide informal fraction experiences in which the part-whole relation is less obvious. For example, have a child folds a pillowcase, towel, or piece of paper in half, then in half again. Explain the idea that the folded portion in the child's hand is actually one-fourth of the original pillowcase because the other three parts are hidden.

◆ Challenge some children to work with materials that cannot be easily cut or folded. For example, challenge a child to divide a wooden block into four equal parts using only two elastic bands. One solution resembles ribbon wrapped around a gift box.

Connections

◆ With the world of the child: When we eat or share food, we often use fractions. For instance, we cut the apple in halves or quarters, we split a banana in half, or we cut the muffin in half to butter it.

◆ With other mathematics: Because of the shapes that result when we cut other shapes into equal portions, fractions are connected closely with shape recognition and informal concepts of area. Sharing, or early knowledge of division, also links with fraction knowledge.

◆ Arts and crafts activities that involve cutting or folding paper often incorporate fractions. Fraction activities also fit easily in broader themes about celebrations or foods.

Process Standards Addressed: Children are introduced to the language of mathematics and use it to *communicate* ideas precisely. They also *solve mathematical problems* that naturally arise in everyday settings.

Benny's Pennies

This activity is adapted from the book *Benny's Pennies* by Pat Brisson (1995).

Goals: Count with understanding and recognize "how many" in small sets of objects

Suggested Context: Reading center

Recommended Age Range: 4–5 years

Materials: *Benny's Pennies* (Brisson 1995); chart paper; five separate collections of ten or more items, such as crayons, fruit counters, small items of doll clothing, small wrapped pieces of chocolate, or goldfish crackers, grouped together in containers; five film canisters or plastic containers with five pennies inside each one; paper lunch bags; marker

Groupings: Whole class, followed by work with groups of five children, or one child and one adult

Description

1. Read *Benny's Pennies* by Pat Brisson.

2. While reading the book, pause and ask questions that will get the children ready to predict and infer using their understanding of number concepts. For example, after page 3, ask the children how many objects they think Benny will need to purchase so that each character in the story, that is, the mother, brother, sister, cat, and dog, will get one gift.

3. After reading the book, ask the children to help you remember what items Benny purchased. Draw a picture of each item on one side of the chart paper. Ask the children to tell you how many pennies Benny had to spend altogether. Draw one penny on the opposite side of the chart paper, and ask the children if that amount is enough. Continue pausing and asking the children if you have enough pennies until you have drawn all five pennies.

4. Draw lines from the pennies on one side of the chart paper to the purchased items on the opposite side of the chart paper to help the children visualize the one-to-one correspondence.

5. Gather a group of three to five children to play the game based on *Benny's Pennies*. Send the other children to centers that they have used previously.

6. Distribute a canister of five pennies to each child. Tell the children that these will be their five pennies to spend on the items you have displayed in the individual containers. Remind them that one item is worth one penny, just as the items were worth one penny in the story *Benny's Pennies*.

7. Instruct the children to count the pennies in their canisters. Observe how the children count the pennies. Refer to the section of this lesson plan called "Expectations" to help you assess the children's counting behaviors.

8. Distribute one empty lunch bag per child. Tell the children to put as many items from the containers into their "grocery bags" as the number of pennies they have in their canisters.

9. Tell the group of children to bring their bags of purchases to you. Pretend to be the cashier. Empty their purchases from the bags. As you pretend to scan one item on the cash register, collect one penny from the child.

10. After each child has gone through the checkout line, give him or her a piece of paper to draw or represent each item purchased. Below each drawing, have the child make a representation of 5 using penny stickers or tally marks. For capable children, distribute new canisters that have more than five pennies.

11. Collect these drawings from each child, and make a class book called *Our Pennies*.

Expectations

◆ Children may create a matching set of objects using perception. The child who quantifies in this manner is using a *global strategy*.

◆ Children may match each item they collect with a corresponding penny to create an equal amount. The child who quantifies in this manner is using a *one-to-one-correspondence strategy*.

◆ Children may count the pennies, then create a corresponding collection of five items by counting out the objects. The child who quantifies in this manner is using a *counting strategy*.

◆ Children may not need to count the pennies or the new set of five items. Instead, they may simply have a mental image of what a set of five looks like and collect the correct amount. A child who quantifies in this manner is using a *subitizing strategy*.

◆ If a child is using a global or one-to-one-correspondence strategy to quantify, he or she may have difficulty with the following counting behaviors:

— Does the child say the correct counting sequence, or does he or she recite the number sequence out of order, for example, "two, three, five, seven"?

— Does the child say a corresponding number word when touching or tagging each object?

— Does the child remember that the last object touched in the set names the entire set? In other words, does the child understand the cardinality principle?

> Mastering the concept of one-to-one correspondence is necessary for young children to learn to count.

Suggestions for Supporting Learners

◆ For the child who has collected too many or too few items to purchase with the five pennies, place one item beside each penny to demonstrate one-to-one correspondence.

◆ Examine the child's collection, and chose from the following questions to guide the child in creating a more accurate matching set of objects:

— Do you have a penny for each item? How can you tell?

— Do you have more [or fewer] items than pennies?

— How many items do you need so that each item can be purchased with only one penny?

— How many more items will you need?

— How many items will you need to take back?

◆ If the child has difficulty drawing her or his purchases, offer alternative forms of representation, such as stickers.

◆ Provide children who have difficulty keeping track of the items they have drawn with five penny or dot stickers to place beside each purchase after they have drawn it.

◆ If a child is learning English as a second language, modify the story by dramatizing it or rephrasing some of the language.

◆ If a child has poor motor skills or orthopedic impairments, you may want to make large cardboard pennies instead of using real coins.

Extensions

◆ If a child is subitizing, that is, recognizing amounts up to five without counting, consider giving the child six to ten pennies with which to purchase a corresponding set of items.

◆ Create a store in the dramatic play center, using a variety of cans, empty cereal boxes, and other items collected by the children from home. Place a cash register in the center along with play money.

◆ Invite children to view the pennies with a magnifier and discover the numbers or letters that are on a penny. Discuss what these letters or numbers mean.

Connections

◆ With the world of the child: Children love to talk about what they would like to buy if they had some money. Make a wish list of things they would like to purchase, such as toys, clothes, collectibles, and so on.

◆ With other mathematics: Children who have demonstrated success with one-to-one correspondence could begin extending their algebraic thinking to two-to-one relationships. For example, ask the children how many purchases they could make with three pennies if two items were worth one penny. Make a table of ordered pairs, for example, one penny for two items; two pennies for four items; three

> Learning to count by using pennies is particularly motivating in a real-life situation, such as shopping.

pennies for six items. Ask the children to find patterns using an input-output rule or relationship.

◆ With other content areas: Counting with pennies lends itself well to economics and social studies. Children could discuss bartering or the occupations they will choose when they grow up.

Process Standards Addressed*:* Children *represent* their purchases by drawing the items purchased with the corresponding pennies. They also engage in *problem solving* to decide whether they have enough pennies to buy their purchases.

Source: *Benny's Pennies*, by Pat Brisson (Glenview, Ill.: Scott, Foresman & Co., 1995).

A Calculator Game: Making Numerals

Goals: To compute using a variety of methods and tools, including objects, mental mathematics, estimation, paper and pencil, and calculators

Suggested Contexts: At home or in a mathematics center

Recommended Age Range: 4–5 years

Materials: A calculator and a book with multidigit page numbers or other print images of multidigit numbers

Groupings: One adult and one child or one adult and a small group of children

Description

Five-year-old Terri asks, "What's 6 plus 10?"

"Sixteen," her mother replies.

"Can't be! The calculator says 7!"

Her mother asks, "What did you enter? Show me."

Terri shows her mother that she pressed [6][+], followed by [0][1][=]. The calculator displays a 7.

Terri's mother explains, "You entered 0, then 1, which is the same as entering 1. If you want to enter 10, you press 1, then 0. The meaning of the number changes depending on how we write it."

1. Give each child a calculator; position yourself so that you can easily see each child's keypad and display.

2. Invite children to explore the calculator by pushing any key and looking at the display. Talk about what they "make the calculator say." Show children how to clear the calculator by using the [clear] key.

3. Talk about how the numbers "look funny" on a calculator display. The lines that make up the numbers are broken. Write the numbers "like a calculator does" next to the printed numbers you are using. Talk about their differences.

4. Help children discover that any single-digit number from 0 to 9 is entered with one key press. Say, "Let's play a game with your calculator! First, show me one finger. Now show me a 1 on your calculator. What key did you press?" Repeat this exercise for the other single-digit numbers, clearing the calculator after each stroke. A deck of cards or a storybook with page numbers may be used to show what the numerals look like.

5. Ask, "Does anyone know another way to make the calculator show 1, 2, 3, … , or 9?" Explain that the calculator has "special" keys that help us show numbers in different ways. Show children the [+] and [=] keys. Ask children to clear their calculators, then key in [1] [+] [2] [=]. Ask what the calculator shows. Then, ask children to clear their calculators and try to show other numbers by using the special keys.

6. Help children discover that any double-digit number from 10 to 99 is entered using two separate key presses; for example, have them press [1], then [0] to enter 10. Ask children, "Show me ten fingers. Does everyone know what the numeral 10 looks like? Help me find page 10 in this storybook." Flip through a children's book that clearly displays page numbers, counting in unison if desired, until you reach page 10. Then direct the children, "Show me 10 on your calculator display. What keys did you press? Does the calculator keypad have a [10] key?"

7. "Show me twelve fingers. [Observe as children flash ten fingers, followed by two fingers.] Where is page 12 in our book? How can we make the calculator show us the number 12? Let's use only the [0] to [9] keys as we did for 10." Repeat this exercise using 21, 19, or numbers of your choice.

8. "When we showed 12 with our fingers, we flashed ten fingers, then two more. The calculator can show us 12 by using 10 and 2 also. Does anyone have an idea about how to press 10 and 2 and get 12?" Someone will probably suggest [1] [0] [2]. If so, invite children to try this sequence. Express surprise that the result, 102, does not look like 12. Say, "I think we need one of those special keys [+, =] to help us." Explore the possibilities.

9. Continue the game by trying other multidigit numbers. "Show me 23 with your fingers and your calculator. First, flash ten fingers, then press [1][0][+]; flash ten fingers again, then press [1][0][+]; flash three fingers, then press [3][=]. What is displayed? What if we try to show 32?" Continue exploring, allowing children to choose numbers and show them on the calculator.

Expectations

◆ Children may not recognize the numerals displayed on the computer as numerals they know. Often, they will say, "The numbers are broken," or "My line is dotted."

◆ Children love to fill the display with lots of numbers. If children appear interested, name the big numbers as they make them.

◆ The level of attention children give to what they enter and what is displayed on the calculator will vary. Some children do not associate the numerals displayed with the keys they press. Operation keys in particular may seem magical to many children. Do not expect that the meanings of the symbols or the relationships between symbols will be obvious to young children.

◆ Many young children can name single-digit numerals, such as 4 or 8. Some children may, randomly or with the help of the adult, name some double-digit numbers that are familiar.

◆ Children may enter digits of multidigit numbers in reverse, moving right to left; for example, 12 may be displayed as 21. Other children may try to show 12 by pressing [1] [0] [2], resulting in 102 on the display.

Suggestions for Supporting Learners

◆ Through questions and conversation, focus the children's attention on what keys are pressed and what symbols are displayed. Play a guessing game to explore what actions create a certain display, and encourage children to watch carefully as you model the actions.

◆ Adult assistance is needed to help children understand and recognize multidigit numerals and, in some instances, the numerals 0–9, when the children enter these numbers on the calculator.. Young children do not automatically recognize 45 as *forty-five*, nor do they necessarily know that the word *twenty-six* is represented by a 2 and a 6. Naming multidigit numbers as children display them on calculators is one way to familiarize children with the spoken names. Another method is to find a corresponding page number or other representation, show it to the children as you name the number, and have them enter what they see into the calculator.

◆ Flashing your fingers or having counters of some type to show amounts enhances children's understanding of numbers. The numbered playing cards, for example, show both the numeral, such as 8, and the number of objects, such as eight hearts. Visual images, such as posters or puzzles, that show the numeral, its name, and its amount also help children develop understanding of numbers.

> Recognizing the numeral displayed on the calculator does not mean that the child understands the amount it represents.

◆ For some children, working with specific multidigit numbers may prove confusing. These children may be more successful if you leave the task open and allow them to explore the number names and values that they choose. The task may also be more manageable if you ask the children to add 10 to other single-digit numbers. For example, you might ask, "What does 6 + 10 show?" or "What does 9 + 10 show?" Discuss what children notice as they enter the numbers into the calculator.

◆ If children have special needs and use special communication devices, they can participate in this activity by using the number functions on these devices.

Extensions

◆ Playing with the counting pattern is often an enjoyable activity for young children and one that is filled with many discovery opportunities. Ask them to clear their calculators and key in [0] [+] [1] [=] [=][=][=][=].... Discuss what they notice. Try other starting numbers.

◆ Children may also be intrigued by explorations with simple number combinations. Have children add 10 and 1, add 11 and 11, add 12 and 21, and so on. Ask children what happens when they add the first nine counting numbers, that is, 1 + 2 + 3 ... + 9. What is the total?

◆ A calculator can be used as the "cash register" in a play store to mimic real-life applications. You and a child may use a store flier to set prices, or the child may charge his or her own prices for imaginary items or toys. You may create pricetags on scraps of paper or stickers and place them on books, toys, and clothes that the child has gathered to "sell."

Connections

◆ With the world of the child: Calculators are visible in the child's home, school, and community environments. They are sometimes available in banks next to automatic teller machines or are used by adults in grocery stores or restaurants.

◆ With other mathematics: Calculators are often used to generate patterns for young children. For example, the +1 pattern described in "Extensions" is a familiar one, and many other patterns, such as + 2, –1, or +10, can be investigated, as well.

◆ With other content areas: Using the page numbers of children's books, particularly anthologies and information books, indirectly connects numeracy and book literacy. Children come to recognize the page numbers and later use that knowledge to consult a glossary or table of contents to find a favorite nursery rhyme or picture.

Process Standards Addressed: Children *create and use representations* to organize, record, and communicate mathematical ideas. If children are unfamiliar with the numerals and the calculator, this activity allows them to build new mathematical knowledge through *problem solving.*

> We highly recommend allowing children to engage in free exploration and play with calculators, along with doing more structured calculator activities. Short conversations about explorations with calculators should also be sprinkled throughout everyday experiences.

The Last Word

COMMENTS FROM TEACHERS ABOUT NUMBER AND OPERATIONS

LOOKING BACK

Where are my students now?

♦ The children enjoyed the Developing Pictures activity. Some focused on the process and others, just on counting. Identifying their understanding from their responses was easy. All were willing to share their ways of counting.

What activities can I change?

♦ I used the doughnut activity while we were traveling in the car. I used colored cereal, and we ate one colored cereal piece when we saw a car that was that color. We had lots of fun and kept saying, "One more!"

How did the children surprise me?

♦ A student came to me asking how to make a 20 on the calculator. I asked him how to make a 10. He said, "A ten and a one." He punched in 0 and 1 and said, "Hey, that's not a ten…that's one." He tried again, pushing 1 and 0, and said, "There, 10!" I asked him how he could make 20 , and he replied, "Oh, a 2 and a 0. Yeah!"

♦ Two of my four-year-old students had difficulty at first with the Developing Pictures activity. After several rounds, they were more successful, and one said, "I already know how to add these counters after practicing for a while!"

♦ I was surprised at how one child responded to the Developing Pictures activity. When she looked under the flap to count how many, she had six bug counters rather than the five she needed. She responded, "This bug snucked into the pile. It doesn't belong!" I thought her response was a pretty creative way to solve the problem and make it right!

LOOKING AROUND

Where else is this content in my room already?

♦ After I used the calculator activity, I found other opportunities for calculator use in my classroom everywhere. I put out a calculator near the morning sign-in sheet. Each child entered a number that told something about himself or herself, recorded the number on the sign-in sheet, then told us all about it later.

◆ *Benny's Pennies* was a favorite activity of many of my students. The film canisters filled with pennies became part of the home center activities, and the children flocked to the home center to spend their money!

◆ My students used the Fraction Food activity often during center choice time. My prekindergarten children loved it and were interested in cutting things "fair!"

What else could I do?

◆ I would like to find more books that address the part-part-whole idea. I never thought about numbers like that, and my children loved the pom-pom toss game.

LOOKING FORWARD

Where do we go from here?

◆ I am going to use the idea of shopping more often after using the *Benny's Pennies* activity. My four-year-olds loved the idea of shopping for gifts for friends, and they loved having pennies to shop with. They were totally engaged during the selection and payment/checkout phases of the activity. Although they seemed to understand the one-to-one relationship between the pennies and the items purchased, some students still seemed surprised when they had too many items in their bags.

What should I start doing?

◆ I have started asking children big questions, such as "Have you found all the ways to show six? How do you know? Are you sure?" Then, I sit back and they surprise me!

Chapter 3
Geometry

THE BIG PICTURE

SELECTED EXPECTATIONS FROM *Principles and Standards for School Mathematics*

> **In prekindergarten through grade 2, all students should—**
>
> - recognize, name, build, draw, compare, and sort two- and three-dimensional shapes;
>
> - describe attributes and parts of two- and three-dimensional shapes;
>
> - investigate and predict the results of putting together and taking apart two- and three-dimensional shapes;
>
> - describe, name, and interpret relative positions in space and apply ideas about relative position;
>
> - find and name locations with simple relationships, such as "near to," and in coordinate systems, such as maps;
>
> - recognize and apply slides, flips, and turns;
>
> - recognize and create shapes that have symmetry;
>
> - create mental images of geometric shapes using spatial memory and spatial visualization;
>
> - recognize and represent shapes from different perspectives;
>
> - relate ideas in geometry to ideas in number and measurement;
>
> - incorporate geometric shapes and structures in the environment and specify their locations.
> (p. 96)

YOUNG CHILDREN'S MATHEMATICAL THINKING ABOUT GEOMETRY

Young children typically learn the names for the following two-dimensional shapes: rectangles, triangles, rhombi, ovals, and circles. They also learn to identify these shapes by sight and touch, such as when the shapes are placed in a "feely bag." Often, children identify items in their environment that are examples of these common shapes. These skills are important for children to acquire, but children should also learn about many other concepts in geometry. This chapter addresses those concepts in the following categories:

- ◆ Shape
- ◆ Locations, directions, and coordinates
- ◆ Visualization and spatial reasoning
- ◆ Transformations and symmetry

Shape

Young children learn about shapes because their environment is composed of shapes. Preschool children are able to identify circles accurately in a collection of shapes that includes circles of various sizes, ovals, a square, and a triangle. Children are less accurate in classifying triangles and rectangles, identifying triangles with an accuracy rate of about 60 percent. They have difficulty with triangles that are different from the typical triangles that they experience (Clements et al. 1999). Often young children think of a triangle as having all sides equal or, at least, two sides equal, with one side in a horizontal orientation. Children often do not classify long, skinny triangles and triangles with three unequal sides as triangles, even though they may say that triangles have three sides and three angles, corners, or points. Children seem to have the general idea that a rectangle has two long sides that are parallel and four corners that are close to 90 degrees. They do not choose squares as rectangles, but many children identify right trapezoids and long, skinny parallelograms with angles near 90 degrees as rectangles.

Children in richer learning environments were able to select examples of the foregoing shapes much more accurately (Clements 1999). In such environments, children investigated shapes by combining, folding, cutting, drawing, and copying them. They measured sides and discussed properties of the shapes. They built shapes using toothpicks and small marshmallows and used string to create triangles and transform them into squares and rectangles. They encountered a much greater variety of each type of shape and learned that a square is a special type of rectangle, just as an equilateral triangle is a special type of triangle. These children experienced shapes actively, explored examples and nonexamples of the various shapes, and engaged in interesting tasks involving shapes.

Children learn about shapes during their preschool years, and their concepts of shapes stabilize as early as age six (Clements 1999). For this reason, their understanding of shapes should be rich and accurate.

Locations, Directions, and Spatial Orientation

Preschool children explore space and learn about the properties and relationships of objects in their environment. Even three-year-olds can make meaningful maps by using landscape toys, such as trees and houses (Blaut and Stea 1974), and kindergarten children can use model furniture to make representations of their classrooms (Siegel and Schadler 1977). Children can usually learn from maps made by others. For example, they are able to learn a pathway through six rooms more accurately from a map than from physically investigating the rooms. Preschool children know that a map represents space but are often unable to identify their locations on a map. They are also unable to put themselves in a different perspective; for example, they may have difficulty identifying what someone else would see from a different location (Uttal and Wellman 1989).

Young children can develop spatial orientation by acting out stories that involve location, direction, distance, and specific objects. Such stories as

> Young children can develop spatial orientation by acting out stories that involve location, direction, distance, and specific objects.

"The Three Billy Goats Gruff," "Little Red Riding Hood," and "Goldilocks and the Three Bears" provide opportunities to use concepts of direction and distance, including *near, far, next to, between, big, little,* and *middle-sized.* Children can make models of the story settings and discuss what the characters see from their locations. These initial components of spatial orientation become more fully developed as children encounter a wide variety of maps in and out of school.

Visualization and Spatial Reasoning

Spatial visualization involves creating mental images of geometric objects, examining the objects mentally, and transforming them. At first, children's mental images of objects are static; they cannot be manipulated (Clements 1999). Later, children are able to move objects mentally, such as when they predict whether a chair will fit into a space in the classroom. They can also rotate an image of a geometric shape to "see" if it matches a similar shape somewhere else on the carpet.

Children's spatial visualization can be developed in preschool settings. Children can be asked to think of a circle and mentally cut it in half or fold the top down to the bottom and flatten the circle, then draw what they "see." Children often use mental imagery when they fill in the outline of a shape with smaller shapes, such as when using tangrams.

Transformations and Symmetry

Four- and five-year-old children can move shapes to determine whether they are identical to other shapes; they slide, rotate, and sometimes even flip the shapes to determine whether they match (Clements 2004). They also use these transformations when they solve puzzles that require them to build a shape from smaller shapes. When children build with geometric shapes or create artistic patterns by folding and coloring paper, they frequently make designs that have line symmetry or rotational symmetry. Some kindergarten children can use symmetry to create the other half of a geometric figure and can identify lines of symmetry in a given figure.

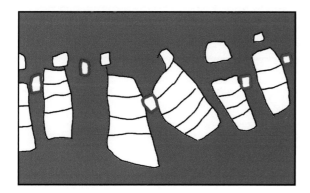

A five-year-old's representation of his block city

GEOMETRY ACTIVITIES

The following table provides a brief description of each activity in the next sections.

NAME OF ACTIVITY	DESCRIPTION	PAGE
Hanny Learns about Making Shapes from the Baby Elephants	Children make shapes with their bodies to match those made by the baby elephants.	59
Construction Creations	Children create many types of constructions, talk about their creations, and represent them.	63
Lots and Lots of Boxes	Children investigate the attributes of rectangular prisms in six different centers.	66
Transformation!	Children "transform" play dough into three different three-dimensional shapes: a rectangular prism, sphere, and cylinder	68
Block-Stacking Game	Children play a game and build tall stacks of three-dimensional shapes.	70
Quilting with Paper	Children create a quilt using only square and rectangular shapes to cover an area completely.	72
Triangle Blocks	Children fill a square block with many two-colored triangular shapes to make a pattern of geometric shapes.	74
Six-Pack Weavings	Children use position words to describe the weavings they create.	77
Shape Steps	Children analyze the attributes of two-dimensional shapes by "stepping the shapes."	79
Where's the Bunny?	Children find a bunny puppet using a map with shape and arrow locators.	81
Mystery Sticks	Children predict and discover the two-dimensional shapes that can be made using a variety of sticks of different sizes.	84

Hanny Learns about Making Shapes from the Baby Elephants

STAGING THE SCENARIO

Bring out the honey-bear stick puppet, and enact the following scenario:

Hanny the Honey Bear: Hello, boys and girls; are you ready for my next adventure in the zoo? I am near where the elephants live. My, oh my, they are big! Look at their giant ears flapping back and forth. Wait, I see six baby elephants over there. Aren't they cute? Hello there, I'm Hanny the Honey Bear. Who are you?

Next bring out the six baby elephant stick puppets to continue the scenario.

Binky, Boo, Bobo, Baba, Beany, and Bart: We're Binky, Boo, Bobo, Baba, Beany, and Bart, and we like to play games. Our parents came from Africa, but we were born in the zoo, and we like it here. We play lots of games together. Watch us play follow the leader.

Hanny the Honey Bear: I watch as they line up, hold onto one another's tails with their trunks, and walk in a straight line. How cute they are as they lumber along, rocking from side to side! Seeing them makes me want to sing.

Bring out the following poem, written on chart paper, as Hanny chants the words:

> *Elephants march in a straight line.*
> *My, oh my, do they look fine.*
> *Trunk to tail, holding tight.*
> *My, oh my, that's quite a sight.*

Hanny the Honey Bear: Can you pretend to walk like an elephant? Show me how you would move your bodies to walk from side to side. Show me how you would swing your trunk. Next show me how you would pretend to be elephants and walk in a straight line. Be sure to make a very straight line, just like the baby elephants. Now Binky, Boo, Bobo, Baba, Beany, and Bart are making a wavy line that curves around. Can you turn your straight line into a curvy line? Good; that line is curvy.

Bring out the following poem, written on chart paper, as Hanny sings:

> *Elephants make a curvy line.*
> *My, oh my, do they look fine.*
> *Trunk to tail, holding tight.*
> *My, oh my, that's quite a sight.*

Binky, Boo, Bobo, Baba, Beany, and Bart: If you liked that, just watch us now. We're going to make a real shape!

Hanny the Honey Bear: Look! The baby elephants are making a shape. They are going 'round and 'round in a circle. They look so funny with their ears flapping around and their bodies swinging from side to side.

Bring out poem, written on chart paper, as Hanny chants the words:

> *Elephants march 'round and 'round,*
> *Making a circle on the ground.*
> *Trunk to tail, holding tight.*
> *My, oh my, that's quite a sight.*

Hanny the Honey Bear: Here is the shape the baby elephants made with their bodies. Can you make the shape in the air with your arms?

Hold up a circle, and have the children make circular arm movements in the air. Have them talk about the attributes of a circle, that is, it is curved, has no straight lines, and has no corners.

Hanny the Honey Bear: Here's another shape that the six elephants made with their bodies. [The teacher holds up the oval shape.] Can you tell me about this shape? I would like to know all about it. Describe it to me.

Hold up an oval, and have the children make an oval in the air. Discuss the similarities and differences between the oval and the circle, including that both are curved, neither has straight lines, and neither has corners, but one makes a round shape and one makes a shape more like that of an egg.

Hanny the Honey Bear: Here is another shape that the six elephants made with their bodies. [The teacher holds up the equilateral triangle.] Can you tell me about this shape? I would like to know all about it. Describe it to me.

Have children talk about the number of sides and corners on the triangle and whether the sides are straight or curved. Ask them whether they know what the shape is called. Have children trace triangles in the air.

Hanny the Honey Bear: Bobo and Bart decided that they wanted to rest a bit. The other four baby elephants are making this shape now.

Hold up a square shape as a "special" kind of rectangle. Have children talk about the number of sides and corners on the square, whether the sides are straight or curved, and whether the sides have the same length or different lengths. Ask them whether they know what the shape is called. Have children trace squares in the air.

> Have the children talk about the attributes of a circle, that is, it is curved, has no straight lines, and has no corners.

Hanny the Honey Bear: Guess what? Bobo and Bart decided that they want to join the game again. The six elephants couldn't make a square, but they could make a different rectangle, one that is not a square. Can you make this shape in the air? You know, now that the elephants worked together to make all these shapes, Binky, Boo, Bobo, Baba, Beany, and Bart have said that they would like to see you pretend to be the baby elephants. Can you be the baby elephants and make the same shapes they did? Be sure to tell us all about each shape and how the shapes are the same or different.

CONDUCTING THE ACTIVITY

Goals: Recognize and describe the attributes of two- and three-dimensional shapes; investigate and predict the results of putting shapes together and taking them apart

Suggested Context: During a lesson

Recommended Age Range: 4–5 years

Materials: Hanny stick puppet and six elephant stick puppets (see templates in appendix C); different paper shapes of acute and equilateral triangles, square, rectangle, circle, and oval; large space for movement; poems about the shapes that the elephants made, written on chart paper

Groupings: Large group or small groups

Description

1. Have the children divide into groups of six or more. Tell them that they will pretend to be the baby elephants making the shapes with their bodies.

2. Hand out a different shape (circle, oval, equilateral triangle, square, or rectangle) to each group. Ask the groups to work together and plan how to make the different shapes with their bodies. While they are planning, have them discuss the characteristics of their shapes.

3. Ask the children to come together as a whole group, and have one group at a time pretend to be the baby elephants and make a shape.

4. The children sitting should describe the shapes made by the other groups, including whether the shapes have straight or curved lines. For shapes with straight sides, the number of sides and corners should be described, and the children should note whether the lines made by the "elephants" are straight enough. The observers can also name the shape.

5. Ask the groups to explain the shapes they made. Did the shape come out the way the group expected it to? What did they need to change to make the shape correctly?

> Ask children to work in groups to plan how to make different shapes with their bodies and to discuss the characteristics of their shapes.

Expectations

◆ You will have to remind children of the attributes of the shapes as they form their models together. Ask them, "How many points are needed? How many straight lines? How can you show that part of the shape? Do you need another person to make your shape? Do you have too many children?"

Suggestions for Supporting Learners

◆ Review and emphasize what the children know about shapes and their attributes.

◆ Help groups of children form the shapes with their bodies as they stand on the floor.

Extensions

◆ Look around the room to find shapes in your environment. Ask children to cut out magazine pictures of objects that have a specific shape. These pictures can be pasted on card stock, labeled with the shape name on top, and used for a shape display in the classroom.

◆ Use large paper clips or other "elephant" manipulatives to model the elephant shapes. Ask children to pretend that the clips are elephants. Determine whether they can make the shapes using the clips in the same way that the elephants did.

Connections

◆ With the world of the child: Children notice the shapes of everyday objects, such as tires, boxes, books, blocks, paper, street signs, and slices of pizza or pie.

◆ With other content areas: Children learn mathematical vocabulary relating to the various shapes and attributes, including such words as *lines, points, angles, curved,* and *straight.*

CONCLUDING THE STORY

Bring out the honey-bear and baby-elephant stick puppets, and enact the story's conclusion.

Hanny the Honey Bear: The baby elephants hug one another in excitement. They lean against one another, with trunks entwined, and this is what they say: [The teacher brings out the following poem on chart paper.]

> *We love your shapes.*
> *We really do.*
> *You've learned our game*
> *Through and through.*

Hanny the Honey Bear: They wave good-bye to me as I set off for another adventure in the big zoo.

Construction Creations

Goals: Investigate and predict the results of putting together and taking apart two- and three-dimensional shapes; describe, name, and interpret relative positions in space, and apply ideas about relative position

Suggested Contexts: Home, school, or any setting with building materials

Recommended Age Range: 3–5 years

Materials: Building materials of any type, such as wooden, foam, or plastic blocks; paper or plastic cups; cardboard boxes of different sizes, including tissue, cereal, or clothing boxes; pipe cleaners; wooden rods; clay

Groupings: Small group or one adult and one child

Description

Four-year-old Jeffrey wants to build a city as a surprise for his family. After 45 minutes of construction, he gathers his family members, their eyes closed, and "presents" his latest creation: a multidimensional, multitiered building complete with symmetry and a driveway leading to the front. The top of Jeffrey's building has two levels, both crowned with flat rectangular blocks supporting triangular pieces. The upper level has three triangular prisims; the lower level, two. When asked why he chose only two triangular prisims for the lower level, Jeffrey responded, "It looks more beautiful that way." For the lower level of the building, Jeffrey chose arches. He demonstrated for the family how his large truck could go under the building. Someone commented that even the smaller car close by could go under the building. Jeffrey replied, "I know that. My first tower had this yellow curve piece [arch] on the very bottom, but it was too short for my bigger truck, so I lifted up the yellow pieces with this blue rectangle to make it higher for my truck. See?"

Two-year-old Amanda enjoyed holding wooden blocks and banging them together. Her mother would say, "You are holding cubes, Amanda." Eventually, Amanda began to notice the names of the shapes, and she might declare "Triangle!" when she was holding a cylinder. Her mother would respond, "That's a cylinder, like a can; here's a triangle" and hand her a flat triangular shape, such as a tangram piece.

1. Facilitate building with three-dimensional shapes. Observe children as they create low buildings and roadways, high towers, entire cities, or specific objects. Talk about what they are building, noting the names of the flat sides of the blocks, such as *circle, square, rectangle,* or *triangle,* or the names of the blocks as a whole, such as *cone, cube, cylinder, box,* or *rectangular prism.* Then discuss the characteristics of the shapes used and which structures were particularly sturdy or weak.

2. Model building creations of your own. For example, you can build a pyramidlike structure by turning paper cups upside down and placing one cup on top of two cups. Elicit help from children for building your creation. Ask, "What do you think I should build?" "What do you think would happen if I tried to put a rectangular block on this triangular block?" or "Why should I not use this block?"

3. Model the appropriate behavior when the creation collapses, for example, "Oh, well. We can do it again!"

4. Allow time and space for constructing. Children need to be able to explore the different kinds of blocks, talk about what they have built, and respond to your constructions.

5. When the creations seem to be completed, ask children whether they would like to save their work in some way. Suggest a photograph, or, if the children seem interested, ask them to draw pictures of what they made.

> Model the appropriate behavior when the creation collapes, for example, "Oh, well. We can do it again!"

Expectations

◆ A child may try to make a tower with a narrow base. Many children do not have the experience to know that the tower will probably fall.

◆ If children have difficulty building with the materials you have given them, select others that may be easier for them to hold or manipulate.

◆ Some children will begin naming their creations right away; others will seem to focus on the building process, and the kind of structure they are creating will change throughout construction.

Suggestions for Supporting Learners

◆ As you build with a child, describe out loud what both of you are doing: "You put that cup on top of the bottom one. This cup is next to that one." Be sure to use position words, such as *top* and *bottom, over* and *under,* and *next to.*

◆ As you help a child build, talk through what you are thinking: "I wonder why this tower is so wobbly? How do you think we could fix it?"

◆ Offer hints or suggestions on how to build; listen to the child's suggestions, as well.

◆ Many children become upset if their structures are destroyed or fall over. Teach them how to react appropriately and to try again.

Extensions

◆ Encourage children to draw pictures of their buildings, just as architects do. Ask them to draw their structures on sheets of butcher paper and roll them up like building plans.

◆ Take photographs of buildings in the children's environment. Place them with the building materials, and suggest that children copy them.

Connections

◆ With the world of the child: Structures surround children, and they are interested in how buildings are put together. Stacking blocks and knocking them down is an engaging activity for young children.

◆ With other mathematics: Measurement principles are in constant use as children examine the height of their towers or the width of a particular creation.

◆ With other content areas: Building gives children direct experience with principles of physical science, such as balance and gravity. Drawing a picture of a finished creation reinforces representation and writing skills.

Process Standards Addressed: Children *solve the problem* of creating structures that match their mental images of what they want to build. They must also select building materials that will stack or that will stay in place.

> Building gives children direct experience with principles of physical science, such as balance and gravity.

Lots and Lots of Boxes

Goals: Recognize, name, build, draw, compare, and sort two- and three-dimensional shapes; describe attributes and parts of two- and three-dimensional shapes

Suggested Contexts: Centers or stations

Recommended Age Range: 4–5 years

Materials: A variety of boxes to serve as models; a box of one-inch cubes; wooden blocks; play dough; waxed paper; blocks in a sock; drawing paper and crayons; a small ramp; a variety of shape models, such as spheres, triangular prisms, rectangular prisms, cubes, cereal boxes, balls, and so on

Groupings: Small groups at centers; whole group at the beginning and end of the lesson

Description

1. Set up the centers as outlined in step 4.

2. Bring children together, and show them two boxes of different sizes. Ask children to tell how the boxes are alike. Encourage them to talk about the "flat sides," or *faces*. Ask how many faces they see. Count the six faces as a group.

3. Show other shape models, and ask children to tell why they are not boxes.

4. Introduce centers. Ask children to rotate to the different centers and to make boxes at each one. The centers are as follows:

   ◆ Inch-cube boxes: Make as many different boxes as possible using the one-inch cubes.

   ◆ Wooden blocks: Make as many different boxes as possible using the wooden blocks.

   ◆ Play dough and waxed paper: Make as many different boxes as possible using the play dough.

   ◆ Shapes in socks: Children use the sense of touch to find boxes hidden among other three-dimensional shapes, such as marbles, inside the socks.

   ◆ Materials for drawing box models: Children use crayons to draw a selected box model on paper.

◆ Ramp and small boxes: Children place boxes at different places on a ramp and watch what happens to them.

◆ Play dough, waxed paper, and wooden blocks: Children flatten out the play dough on the waxed paper. They then select one rectangular-prism block and press all its faces into the play dough.

5. As children work in the centers, circulate among them and ask, "What have you made [or drawn]? How do you know it is a box? Show me the faces. What would fit in the box you have made? Are there any shapes you have made that are *not* boxes? How do you know?" After children have visited all or most of the centers, call them back to the whole group and ask the questions about boxes again. List all their discoveries. Show them shapes that are boxes and ones that are not boxes. Ask them to tell which shapes are boxes and to explain why.

Expectations

◆ Children will enjoy some centers more than others. After introducing them to all the centers, allow them to choose where they want to spend their time.

◆ Children may draw rectangles rather than boxes. You will need to ask children to tell you about the "other rectangles" they see on the box models.

◆ Children love to learn big words. Share with them the name of the typical box shape, which is called a *rectangular prism* because it is a three-dimensional figure with six rectangular faces.

Suggestions for Supporting Learners

◆ Initially, children will build "boxes" that are not boxes. Their constructions will have parts that stick out or consist of small boxes on top of larger ones. You will need to emphasize the idea that boxes have flat faces on the sides.

◆ Children will often say "square" or "rectangle" when they are showing you their boxes. Say, for example, "Yes, the face of the box is a rectangle. The whole box is called a rectangular prism."

◆ Talk about the word *face* by pointing out that people's faces are bumpy but that a box has flat faces.

Extensions

◆ Children can investigate other three-dimensional shapes using many of these same ideas.

◆ Other mathematical terms can be introduced to children. For example, shapes that "look like cans" are *cylinders*, and shapes that "look like balls" are *spheres*.

Connections

◆ With the world of the child: Children love to investigate objects by choice and to formulate their own conjectures using their experiences.

◆ With other content areas: The generalizations required in science relate directly to this activity. Children observe using their senses of touch and sight and make hypotheses about what they investigate.

Process Standards Addressed: Children *communicate* the attributes of boxes; they *represent* their findings with clay or drawings; and they *reason* to determine whether a shape is or is not a box.

Transformation!

Goals: Recognize and represent shapes from different perspectives; recognize, name, build, draw, compare, and sort two- and three-dimensional shapes

Suggested Context: As a table activity

Recommended Age Range: 3–5 years

Materials: Enough play dough or clay for each child; three-dimensional models to represent various shapes, such as a box to represent a rectangular prism or cube, a ball to represent a sphere, and a can to represent a cylinder; one sheet of waxed paper or a plastic plate for each child to use as a working surface

Groupings: Small group or one adult and one child

Description

1. Give children time to work with the play dough and make any shapes they wish.

2. Next talk about the word *transform*, and ask children to tell what they know about objects that transform. Note that most young children have played with toys known as Transformers. These toys change from one form to another with just a few motions.

3. Explain that everyone, including any adult helpers, will make shapes, then change them into different shapes when the teacher calls, "Transform!"

4. Place the sphere, represented by a ball, in the center of the table. Ask children to make a ball using play dough.

5. Talk about what children are doing as they roll the play dough and try to smooth out all the bumps and ridges.

6. When everyone's play-dough shape looks similar to the ball, call out "Transform!" and place the rectangular prism, represented by a box, in the center of the table.

7. Again model the transformation with your ball of play dough, talking about the methods you are using to change the shape. Talk about the smooth faces on the play dough and the edges and vertices.

8. Next call out "Transform!" and place the cylinder, represented by a can, in the center of the table.

9. Again model the transformation with your ball of play dough, describing what you are doing as you roll the sides to smooth them out and flatten the ends.

10. Finally, call out "Transform!" and let the children make any shapes they choose. They should then describe their shapes using their own words.

Expectations

◆ Many children will work hard to make the shapes. Their shapes will probably not look as finished as yours, but they will be able to feel the results easily.

◆ Most children will want to touch the model shape as well as their peers' creations. Teachers should allow students to feel the shapes and their faces and edges.

Suggestions for Supporting Learners

◆ Some children may become frustrated when they try to make a shape that looks like the rectangular-prism model. Help them mold the clay, talking about what you are doing as you make edges or smooth out sides. If appropriate, you might also give these children plastic knives to use in cutting the edges.

◆ Some children will listen only to your words and will not contribute any descriptive terms of their own. Encourage them to tell what they are doing using their own words by commenting on their transformations.

Extensions

◆ Use more unusual shapes for the transformation activities. A square pyramid, a triangular prism, or a hemisphere are interesting and serve as wonderful examples of three-dimensional shapes.

◆ Give children many opportunities to hold and move three-dimensional shapes in their hands. If possible, they should be able to feel models made of different materials. Provide many opportunities to model with clay, as well.

Connections

◆ With other content areas: Children's work with play dough is an important part of art and creative pursuits. Three-dimensional sculptures often use geometric shapes to form a variety of models.

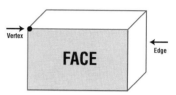

Rectangular prism

Square pyramid

Triangular prism

Hemisphere

Process Standards Addressed: Children *communicate* their ideas and descriptions as they are working. Further, they *represent* the three-dimensional shapes with clay.

Block-Stacking Game

Goals: Investigate and predict the results of putting together and taking apart two-and three-dimensional shapes

Suggested Contexts: Floor area or block center

Recommended Age Range: 3–5 years

Materials: A variety of blocks of different sizes, shapes, and types of materials, such as wood and cardboard; die labeled with one to six pips, or dots, for four- and five-year olds and with one to three pips for three-year-olds; red and blue construction paper

Groupings: Small group, parent working with child, or two children working together

Description

1. Show the blocks, and allow children to manipulate blocks and build their own structures. Show the die, and talk about how to throw it and what pips, or dots, to count.

2. After the children have experimented for a while, tell them that you are going to play a game that will allow them to build tall stacks. Explain that everyone who is playing will get at least two turns to help build a red stack and a blue stack. Explain that sometimes the red stack will get taller and sometimes the blue stack will get taller.

3. The first player throws the die, then selects the number of blocks that are shown on the die. The player also selects either the blue paper or the red on which to build his or her stack. When a player has success in stacking blocks on top of each other, everybody in the group will whisper "Yes!" with their thumbs up. When some blocks fall off, the blocks will be returned to the tub, and everybody in the group will shrug their shoulders, lift their hands outward, and say, "Oh, well!" meaning that they will just keep trying.

4. The game begins with the child who has the shortest little finger. Play continues in a rotation, with each child throwing the die, selecting that number of blocks, and choosing either the red stack or the blue stack to build on.

5. After each turn, ask, "Which stack is taller? Which blocks work well? Which blocks fall off?" Before each turn, ask children, "What do you think will happen? Why do you think so? Could the block be turned another way? What block should you start with? What block should go on top?" When children are counting out the blocks, ask, "How many pips do you see? How do you know? How many more blocks do you need to have enough? How do you know you have the right number?"

6. When everyone has had the same number of turns, the game is over.

Expectations

◆ Children love this game and will continue to play it in the block center after learning it in a small-group setting. Children will begin to improve their strategies dramatically over time.

◆ This activity is an excellent one to use for assessment. Often you will be surprised that some children select three-dimensional shapes that will not stack easily. Their faces show surprise when the stack falls. Others seem to have a knack for selecting blocks and orienting them in "stackable" positions. Specifically, triangular prisms are excellent blocks because they stack well if their triangular faces are placed down on the tower. If placed with a rectangular face down, they do not stack well.

◆ Some children are also good at expressing their predictions verbally. Their vocabulary is clear and well defined. Others have difficulty expressing what they think, but by watching their behaviors, you will often be able to understand what they are thinking about the problem.

Suggestions for Supporting Learners

◆ Children get very enthusiastic about building the stacks and have difficulty waiting for their turns. You will probably need to emphasize repeatedly the idea of playing fairly and the fact that everyone will get the same number of turns.

◆ Some children become upset when the stacks fall over. Continue to have children repeat, "Oh, well!" and remind them that they can still build again. Also, remember to say "Yes!" and give the thumbs-up for every block or leave it in place that is added and stays on the tower.

◆ Frequently, one child will put an upside-down cone or a triangular prism at the top of the structure on his or her turn. The child believes that this type of block should be on top. When the next player tries to add to the stack, however, he or she will have difficulty continuing to build. Make a rule that children can take the top block off to build when their turn comes. Whether to remove the top block or leave it in place is the player's choice.

◆ Some children try to place spheres, cones, and triangular prisms in their stacks, although many others know that the stack will fall. Allow the stacks to fall, model the "Oh, well!" disposition, and make comments about the blocks that work best.

◆ Encourage children to ask their peers to help them decide which blocks work best for stacking.

◆ Some children need help counting the pips on the die, whereas others just "know" how many the die shows. For those who need help counting the pips, talk about them in groups and touch each pip as it is counted. For example, a showing of five could be described as "four in each corner and one in the middle."

Extensions

◆ This game can be expanded using two dice. One die tells how many blocks to stack, and the other die tells how many blocks to use for each level. The structures become quite detailed using this method, and balance becomes very important.

◆ Using a variety of blocks is an interesting way to extend this activity. Triangular prisms or square pyramids are excellent shapes to use and require children to engage in problem solving to find the appropriate orientations.

◆ Photos can be taken of the largest stacks, and children can tell about the stack that was created and why they think it grew high without toppling.

Connections

◆ With the world of the child: Many children enjoy working in the block center, whereas others do not seem to find this center interesting. Playing this game seems to encourage reluctant builders.

◆ With other mathematics: Combining number with building is an obvious connection of this game with mathematics. Further, the comparison words that children use as they discuss the stacks relate directly to measurement concepts.

◆ With other content areas: The "block-stacking game" fosters oral communication by encouraging children to advise their peers about what blocks to select and to share their ideas. In addition, the game enhances socialization skills by encouraging children to give a thumbs-up for everyone who stacks some blocks and to simply shrug when the stacks fall.

Quilting with Paper

Goals: Recognize, name, build, draw, compare, and sort two- and three-dimensional shapes; investigate and predict the results of putting together and taking apart two- and three-dimensional shapes

Suggested Context: Art center

Recommended Age Range: 4–5 years

Materials: One 18-by-12-inch piece of paper for each student; rectangles and squares cut from multicolored construction paper to the following dimensions: 9 by 9 inches, 4.5 by 4.5 inches, 4.5 by 9 inches, 3 by 3 inches, 3 by 4.5 inches, and 3 by 9 inches; paste; markers; cloth quilt (optional)

Groupings: One adult and one child, small group, whole group

Description

1. Explain that the children are going to make a quilt. Discuss the meaning of the word *quilt* and how quilts are used. If possible, show a real cloth quilt and discuss the smaller sections and how they fit together.

2. Begin a discussion about the different shapes, sizes, and colors that make up the quilt. Talk about the "special rectangles that we call *squares*," and identify any squares that are found in the cloth quilt. Also, identify any rectangles that are not squares. Include in the discussion the identification and meaning of a *side* and a *corner*.

3. Using a blank sheet of paper and several of the colored shapes, model many ways that the quilt can be put together. Say, "Pick a corner of your paper, and remember to start at the top. Add your shapes by placing a new one right next to the first shape. Keep adding shapes until your quilt is finished. This activity is like making a puzzle; you have to make sure that you have picked the right size shape to make it fit."

4. After you have modeled the procedure for making a paper quilt, distribute a blank sheet to each child with a large selection of the colored-paper pieces. Ask children to choose shapes and glue them down until their quilts are completely covered with colored paper.

5. When their blank papers are completely filled, children can make decorative patterns on each piece of their quilts using felt-tip markers. Children may also write the letters of their names in the rectangles of their quilts.

6. As the individual quilts are completed, collect and display them on a bare wall to create a large class quilt.

Expectations

◆ Children usually work hard to make sure that their pieces fit exactly. They often select pieces that are too big or too small for the space available. Encourage them to keep trying and to paste down the pieces only when they are satisfied with their quilt designs.

◆ Children are proud of the finished product. A child may point out his or her quilt on the large quilt and tell how it was made.

> Discuss the different shapes, sizes, and colors that make up the quilt. Include the identification and meaning of a *side* and a *corner*.

Suggestions for Supporting Learners

◆ If children leave large empty spaces on their quilt pieces, show them how to slide the pieces together to make sure that the quilt has no "holes." Remind them to "slide" the pieces into the corners so that they fit perfectly.

◆ If a child's shapes become jumbled before they are pasted down, help the child get the shapes back into place and comment on his or her persistence.

Extensions

◆ Play a guessing game with the class quilt. Ask a child to tell you about his or her quilt piece using color or shape words. Try to guess which piece the child created from the description. Repeat the procedure with other children.

◆ Cut some square or rectangular paper pieces into triangles, and have the children make different quilts.

Connections

◆ With the world of the child: Children love to hear stories about their families, the teacher's family, and other cultures. Quilts are often part of those stories. The class quilt, if decorated by students, could serve to tell a story about the class.

◆ With other content areas: The art of quilting is well known. Compare the class quilt with others found in art books or folklore, and discuss the similarities and differences.

Process Standards Addressed: Children use *problem solving* to fit the colored pieces onto the quilt rectangle to cover it completely. They then *communicate* about their quilts with their peers or an adult.

Triangle Blocks

Goals: Investigate and predict the results of putting together and taking apart two-dimensional shapes; recognize and apply slides, flips, and turns

Suggested Contexts: As a table activity or in the art center

Recommended Age: 5 years

Materials: Two different colors of 3-by-3-inch sticky notes, paste, one 6-by-6-inch sheet of white paper

Groupings: Large or small groups

Description

1. Distribute two sticky notes to each child, one of each color.

2. Demonstrate how to fold the sticky note with the adhesive side inside to make a triangle from the square.

3. Ask children to make triangles out of both squares. Model the method for redoing a triangle that does not exactly match by pulling it apart and folding it again.

4. Show the white paper, and explain that the paper is to be completely covered with colored triangles; no spaces should be left on the white paper. Ask children how many triangles they predict they will need to completely cover the paper. Give children the number of notes they predict they will need. Distribute more if they need them.

5. Have children fold and place triangles on the page, organizing them to make a beautiful square block.

6. When children have arranged the triangles as they wish, they can paste them on the paper.

7. Talk about the colored patterns or new shapes that are made.

8. Count the number of triangles needed to cover the entire page.

9. Display the square blocks by attaching them to a large piece of butcher paper. Ask individual children to describe their blocks. Ask other children to identify the blocks from the descriptions.

Expectations

◆ Most children will be able to cover the entire piece of paper, but they may have difficulty beginning the picture. Sometimes they will start with the middle of the page rather than along the edges.

◆ Initially children will not make patterns with their triangles. They will just place the triangles in a seemingly random order. With some suggestions, they will begin to make patterns and often exhibit delight when they see their patterns.

Suggestions for Supporting Learners

◆ Some children have difficulty folding the sticky notes so that the edges match accurately. Lend support by separating the squares and allowing children to try again. If the paper gets too damaged, discard it and provide a fresh note to start again.

◆ If children have difficulty covering 6-by-6-inch squares, use 3-by-3-inch squares to begin.

◆ Some children may have difficulty completely covering the paper squares. Guide them as they position their triangles, modeling the actions and using the words *slide, flip,* and *turn.*

◆ Some children may complete this activity easily. Before they paste down their pattern, ask them to make another pattern with their triangles.

◆ Many children have difficulty describing their paper squares. Encourage them to tell "what your picture looks like" or to describe "the top" or "the bottom."

Extensions

◆ Use 9-by-9-inch squares of paper rather than 6-by-6-inch squares.

◆ Use three different colors of sticky notes.

◆ Fold or cut triangles in half to create smaller triangle pieces.

Connections

◆ With the world of the child: Children often notice patterns and shapes in their environment. As they make their squares, they may be able to talk about other patterns they have seen that are similar to the ones they are creating.

◆ With other mathematics: Patterns and algebraic thinking are inherent connections with this activity. The colors of the triangles naturally make patterning a possibility and forge a strong connection between geometry and algebra.

◆ With other content areas: Shapes and patterns are often used in art. This activity offers a natural connection between mathematics and the visual arts.

Process Standards Addressed: Children use *problem-solving* skills as they flip, turn, or slide the triangles into place to completely cover the square. They also *communicate* descriptions of their triangle blocks to others using mathematical language.

Six-Pack Weavings

Goals: Describe, name, and interpret relative positions in space; apply ideas about relative position

Suggested Context: Art center

Recommended Age Range: 4–5 years

Materials: Several sets of plastic six-pack rings per child; art materials, such as colored paper, straws, feathers, twigs, yarn in different lengths, pipe cleaners, strips of cloth, ribbons, socks, shoelaces, twist ties; paper mat cut into strips and construction-paper strips for weaving; heavy cardboard mat with triangle edges; tongue depressors for weaving tools

Groupings: One adult with a small group of children or one adult and one child

Description

1. Give each child a set of plastic rings from a beverage six-pack or a weaving mat of your choice. Pause for a few minutes to encourage children to examine the rings and share what they know about them. Acknowledge their statements and explorations, for example, counting the number of rings, seeing if their hands will fit through the holes, talking about their own experiences with these materials, and so on.

2. Show the other art materials. Explain that weaving can be done by putting things over and under the rings.

3. Place the materials for weaving on the table. Select one, and demonstrate weaving it through a set of rings. Use such words as *in, out, over,* and *under* to describe what you are doing.

4. As the children weave, work alongside them. Comment on what they are doing. Encourage them to describe and show to others at the table what they are doing .

5. Midway through the activity, tell the children that many other holders can be used for weaving. If you have noticed children weaving things in and out of a fence in the yard, spokes in a bicycle wheel, and so on, mention these activities to them as examples of weaving. Show children the paper mats with the precut strips, and tell them that they can also use those strips for weaving if they like.

6. Encourage the children to turn their weavings in different directions— upside down, sideways, back to front—and describe what they see.

7. At cleanup time, encourage children to sort the leftover materials into their original containers.

Encourage children to turn their weavings in different directions—upside down, sideways, back to front—and describe what they see.

Expectations

◆ Children will explore the six-pack rings in different ways, especially at first. For example, they may hold them up to their eyes and call them "glasses." Others will say that the rings come from the tops of soda cans. Some will count the number of rings or use them as trays for sorting materials.

◆ Some children might fasten two or more rings together to make a large surface for weaving.

◆ Some children might weave a few items into a set of six-pack rings, then start a new set. Others might include many materials in each weaving.

◆ Some children may have difficulty following the over-and-under pattern. Repeat and model the actions as you work on a weaving pattern.

Suggestions for Supporting Learners

◆ As the children begin to use the materials, note and comment on the different things they do. Continue to use position words, such as *behind* and *in front of, above* and *below, forward* and *back,* and *through.*

◆ Ask questions that encourage children to use spatial language, for example, "How did you get this yarn to connect to the ring?" or "I see that you took a piece of red yarn next. Where will you put it?"

◆ Comment on any patterns the children create, for example, alternating rows of color or texture.

◆ Because the plastic holes are large, children may have difficulty weaving with short pieces of the art materials. Encourage them to use the large pieces first, then weave in the smaller pieces.

Extensions

◆ Add extra six-pack rings and sturdy paper with precut slits to the art area. Make sure to maintain a supply of pipe cleaners, paper and cloth strips, varieties of yarn, and so on.

◆ Hang a sign on the parent bulletin board asking parents to save the rings from beverage six-packs and encouraging them to bring in scrap materials that the children can use for weaving.

◆ Play over-and-under games outside.

◆ Bring in fabric with obvious weave structures, and have children describe how the yarns intersect. Look at fabrics under a magnifying glass to see how they are constructed.

Connections

◆ With the world of the child: Children see and touch fabric in clothing and household furnishings every day. Learning to weave connects children with visual arts and culture in their communities.

> Learning to weave connects children with visual arts and culture in their communities.

◆ With other content areas: This activity encourages children's creativity and the development of a sense of aesthetics. Children share materials and may choose to collaborate on projects, thereby developing social skills. The act of weaving promotes fine-motor skills, such as eye-hand coordination.

Process Standards Addressed: Children create weavings of their choice and *communicate* the process using their own words.

Source: "Six-Pack Weavings" was contributed by the High/Scope Educational Research Foundation, Early Childhood Division, directed by Ann S. Epstein. The activities are adapted from *100 Small-Group Experiences: The Teacher's Idea Book #3* by Michelle Graves (Ypsilanti, Mich.: High/Scope Press, 1997).

Shape Steps

Goals: Recognize, name, compare, and analyze characteristics and properties of two- and three-dimensional geometric shapes; describe attributes and parts of two- and three-dimensional shapes

Suggested Context: During a lesson

Recommended Age Range: 4–5 years

Materials: Masking tape placed on the floor to form a variety of shapes, such as those pictured below; a constantly confused puppet, Mr. Mixup; music (optional)

Preparation Suggestions: Make several large masking-tape shapes on the floor near your circle-time area or, if you prefer, in a gym area or outdoors. Two suggestions for the arrangement of these shapes are shown below. Notice the "tricky" shapes in each of these two groups, for example, the shapes on the left that look like triangles but are not.

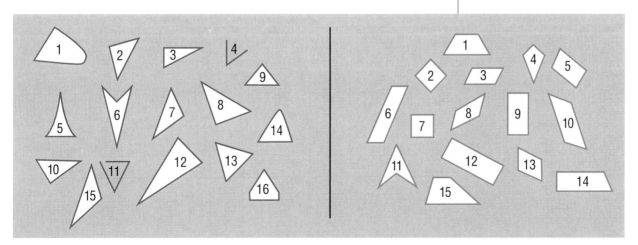

Groupings: Small groups or one adult and one child

Description

1. Show children the shapes you taped to the floor. Ask them to "touch a triangle with your toes," reminding them that the shapes they choose must have the right "parts," or attributes. You might also have children dance around as music is playing, then touch a triangle when the music stops.

2. Discuss the reasons for choosing or not choosing certain shapes. Counting the sides together helps children correct themselves.

3. Children might also trace around the triangles with their fingers. Discuss the fact that the finger moves in a straight line, then "turns on a point," then moves straight and "turns on a point" again, repeating that pattern a total of three times.

4. On a different day, repeat steps 1–3, asking children to first touch a square, a rectangle, or some other class of shape.

5. As children are able, ask them to step on a side or a corner of a rectangle.

Expectations

◆ Children may have difficulty identifying unusual shapes, such as "long, skinny" triangles or rectangles. Help them count the sides, and point out that these shapes have all the attributes of the triangle or rectangle.

◆ Children may have difficulty distinguishing tricky shapes, such as shape 11 on the left on the previous page, which is almost closed, from correct examples of the shape classes.

Suggestions for Supporting Learners

◆ For younger children or children who are having difficulty with the activity, at first omit the tricky shapes, such as shape 5, a triangular shape with curved sides in the first section. Instead, present only simple triangles, rectangles, and circles.

◆ Accept any language the children use to describe the shapes, and model such phrases as *three sides* or *three angles* as you restate their ideas.

◆ For shapes that have right angles, such as the square and rectangle, show children how to hold the thumb and first finger to form a right-angle L and have them test shapes with their "L hands."

◆ As children become more confident, introduce more varied shapes. Challenge children by asking why they did not select a certain shape. For example, when asked to touch a rectangle, ask a child who correctly avoided touching a parallelogram without right angles, such as shapes 6, 10, or 13 on the right on the previous page, why he or she avoided those shapes.

Extensions

◆ Play "Mr. Mixup Messes Up Shape Step." Introduce the confused puppet Mr. Mixup, who talks in a goofy voice. Have Mr. Mixup try to step on a rectangle but instead step on a triangle. Ask children to help Mr. Mixup by explaining which shape is which. Then have Mr. Mixup step on a "tricky" shape that is close to a rectangle but is not. Help children describe the specific attribute that confused Mr. Mixup.

◆ Later, have Mr. Mixup try to step on the side of a rectangle but instead step on the corner. Ask children to help Mr. Mixup by explaining the words *side* and *corner*.

Connections

◆ With the world of the child: Music is an important part of a child's world, and children love to learn by using their bodies.

◆ With other content areas: Learning vocabulary, which is a significant part of this activity, is essential to success in language arts and reading.

Process Standards Addressed: Children *communicate* their *reasoning* throughout this activity as they demonstrate their understanding of geometric vocabulary.

Source: The time to prepare this material was partially provided by National Science Foundation (NSF) research grant ESI-9730804, "Building Blocks—Foundations for Mathematical Thinking, Pre-Kindergarten to Grade 2: Research-Based Materials Development." Any opinions, findings, and conclusions or recommendations expressed in this publication are those of the author and do not necessarily reflect the views of the NSF. The activity is borrowed from one curriculum product, DLM Express Math Resource Package (Clements and Sarama 2003).

Where's the Bunny?

Goals: Find and name locations that illustrate simple direction relationships, such as *near to*; find and name locations in coordinate systems, such as maps

Suggested Contexts: As part of the classroom routine. This lesson is an event that may happen weekly. Children search for the new puppet or stuffed animal that is added to the class each week using the location skills emphasized in this lesson.

Recommended Age Range: 3–5 years

Materials: Stuffed animal or puppet, unit cubes to represent food, map made on butcher paper as described below, *The Secret Birthday Message* (Carle 1986)

Preparation Suggestions: Hide the stuffed animal or puppet somewhere in the classroom. Make a map that contains at least three stopping places before the hiding place of the animal is located. The map should also have a star to show where the path begins and include at least two classroom landmarks to give children an idea of how the classroom is represented. Each stopping place should have a geometric shape that can be located on a real object in the class, as well as one "food" cube. A sample map might look similar to the one shown at the left. The long rectangle is the top of the reading table; a unit cube representing food is under the table. The triangle is the side of the art easel; a unit cube representing food is hidden behind one side. The cylinder is the wastebasket; a unit cube representing food is hidden inside. The bunny is hiding in the corner under the coat rack.

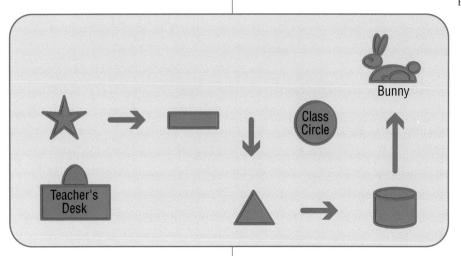

Groupings: Whole group

Description

1. Read *The Secret Birthday Message* (Carle 1986), a story about a little boy who receives a special map to help him find his birthday present, a new puppy. Pay particular attention to the map on the back page of the book.

2. Explain that a new class puppet or animal has been hidden in the room and that the class must find it. Display the map, and ask children to interpret the symbols.

3. Ask children to talk about what the different parts of the map mean. Discuss the arrows, the shape pictures, the star, and the word *bunny*. Locate the class circle and the teacher's desk. Use location words, such as *next to, close to, under, over,* and others in the children's vocabulary.

4. Select one child to stand and go to the starred place shown on the map. Ask children to use words to help the first child find the location represented by the star. Emphasize that the star is not actually on the floor or anywhere else in the classroom; rather, it is a symbol that tells people who are using the map where to start.

5. Direct the child to locate a rectangular-shaped object and to look for the food cube.

6. When the first child finds the food, the activity continues with another child acting as the searcher and the rest of the class helping to direct and read the map.

7. After the bunny is found, review the map and the path of the searchers. Review the shapes found, and use order words to describe the steps of the search; for example, you might say, "First, we found the star; second, we found the rectangle," and so on.

Expectations

♦ Children will become enthusiastic when they see the map displayed. They will try to locate the animal first before following the map from start to finish. The teacher should explain that without the food, the bunny cannot be "found."

♦ Children often ignore the landmarks, in this example, the teacher's desk and the class circle, shown on the map to help them locate their positions. Emphasize the importance of using these clues.

♦ Children's lack of vocabulary may hamper their ability to give clear directions to their peers. Continue to rephrase their ideas and restate their directions using more formal geometric and location terms.

Suggestions for Supporting Learners

♦ If children have difficulty finding the beginning point or the positions of the shaped objects, turn the map so that it is oriented in the same direction as they are sitting or place a stick figure or figures directly on the map to help them visualize their positions on the paper.

♦ If children have difficulty following the arrow directions, do the same activity outside or in a large area. Ask the whole class to "walk the map" as they search for the bunny. Talk about how you are moving "closer to the trees," "next to the swings," and so on.

Extensions

♦ The maps can be posted on the wall for children to revisit frequently. If they show interest, children can make their own maps and the class can "read" them and find where other objects are hidden.

♦ Children can bring other maps to school, and the class can identify landmarks. Often the school map can be enlarged, and children can practice going to the cafeteria or to the bus line by "reading" the map. They can also make a map with arrows to tell a new classmate how to go to the library or the play area.

Connections

◆ With the world of the child: Children love to be detectives and find objects. This activity allows them to use their geometric skills to practice their "detective work."

◆ With other content areas: This activity and the geometry skills it fosters connect with the skills of map reading learned in social studies.

Process Standards Addressed: The process of representation is important in this activity. Children use the map representation and spatial vocabulary to help locate an object.

Source: *The Secret Birthday Message,* by Eric Carle (New York: Harper-Collins, 1991).

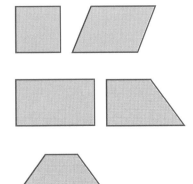

Quadrilaterials

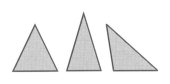

Triangles

Mystery Sticks

Goals: Investigate and predict the results of putting together and taking apart two- and three-dimensional shapes; describe, name, and interpret relative positions in space and apply ideas about relative position

Suggested Contexts: Discovery center and teaching lesson at the end of the activity

Recommended Age Range: 4–5 years

Materials: Craft sticks, straws, or lollipop sticks; paper lunch bags labeled with numerals; cards with two-dimensional representations of polygons (e.g., equilateral, obtuse, and isosceles triangles; rectangle; square rectangle; trapezoid; irregular quadrilateral); play dough

Groupings: Small groups or one child and one adult, followed by a whole-group lesson

Description

1. Make an assortment of sticks or straws cut to lengths of 2 inches, 4 inches, 6 inches, and 8 inches.

2. Place the following combinations of these sticks into corresponding lunch bags, each labeled with a separate numeral 1–7:

   ◆ Bag 1: one 2-inch stick and two 6-inch sticks for the isosceles triangle

   ◆ Bag 2: one 2-inch stick, one 4-inch stick, and one 6-inch stick for the obtuse triangle

- Bag 3: three 4-inch sticks for the equilateral triangle

- Bag 4: two 4-inch sticks and two 8-inch sticks for the rectangle

- Bag 5: four 6-inch sticks for the square rectangle

- Bag 6: two 4-inch sticks, one 2-inch stick, and one 6-inch stick for the trapezoid

- Bag 7: one 2-inch stick, one 4-inch stick, one 6-inch stick, and one 8-inch stick for the quadrilateral

3. Before placing these bags in the discovery center, show them to the students and explain that each bag contains a different set of sticks of various sizes. Tell the children that they will create different shapes with these sticks by putting them together so that each shape is a closed figure. Show the class that the play dough can be used to hold the ends of the sticks together.

4. Remind the children that the sticks in each bag should not be mixed with the sticks in other bags. Color-coding the sticks to match each bag will help keep the sets organized; for example, place a set of red sticks in bag 1 with a red dot sticker affixed to the bag, a set of blue sticks in bag 2 with a blue dot sticker affixed to the bag, and so on.

5. Use an assortment of polygon representations on laminated cards to help students predict what shapes they can make with the sticks in their bags. Encourage students to match each card to the bag that they think has the right set of sticks to create the polygon on the card.

6. When the children have found all the possible ways to correctly arrange the sticks to create closed figures with each point meeting at the endpoint on the sticks, encourage them to draw the shapes on paper or copy them using another set of sticks and glue from the art center.

7. While a small group is working at the center, ask each child to justify his or her thinking using the following probing questions:

- How do you know that the sticks in your bag will make the shape shown on the card?

- What do you notice about the sticks in your bag? How many sticks are in the bag? Are they all the same size, or are some different sizes?

- Can you think of another way to put this same set of sticks together to make a different shape?

- Can you tell me how to make the shape you just made without letting me look at your shape?

8. When every child has had an opportunity to work at this center during the week, review the activity with the whole class. Pose some of the following questions to encourage discussion:

- What did you notice when you put the sticks in the bags together?

- Were some of your predictions true? Why or why not?

- What were the names of some of the shapes you made?

> Ask each child to justify his or her thinking by asking probing questions.

◆ Did you find more than one way to arrange one set of sticks from the same bag?

◆ What are some shapes that we have talked about that we were not able to make with these sticks? Why?

Expectations

◆ Some children might eliminate one stick from a bag with four sticks to create a more familiar shape, especially if the children are having difficulty arranging all the sticks to meet at their endpoints to form a quadrilateral. This problem arises particularly with the rectangle because each pair of sides must be parallel to the other.

◆ Some children may try to join the sticks without matching them at their endpoints. For example, a child may want to make a triangle with equal sides out of two 6-inch sticks and one 2-inch stick; such an arrangement can be made if the sticks are connected in the middle rather than at the endpoints.

◆ Some children may use other names for the isosceles and obtuse triangles. They may say that these shapes are not "good" triangles or that they are not triangles at all.

Suggestions for Supporting Learners

◆ If a child eliminates sticks from the set or does not match them up at endpoints, show the child a picture of the corresponding polygon. Ask the child to use all the sticks without any ends protruding so that his or her shape looks just like the polygon on the card.

◆ On the floor or on the wall, arrange all the shapes that the children made from the mystery sticks. Ask children to classify these shapes into "is" and "is not" categories. Ask them to explain the reasons that some of the shapes do not belong in one category. Ask them to explain how the shapes are alike and different. List these attributes on chart paper.

Extensions

◆ Make a class book that shows all the possible ways to make shapes with three lines and three corners. Title the book *The Many Ways to Make a Triangle*. Make another book for all the possible ways to make shapes with four lines and four corners. Title this book *The Many Ways to Make a Quadrilateral*.

◆ When the children become sufficiently familiar with making these polygons using the suggested assortments of sticks, play the game "what shape am I?" using only verbal clues.

Connections

◆ With other mathematics: As the children compare the sizes of the sticks, they are beginning to understand measurable attributes of length. They are also ordering and comparing the lengths of the sticks to solve problems.

> Ask children to classify their shapes into "is" and "is not" categories and to explain their reasoning.

Process Standards Addressed: Children are involved in *problem solving* when they predict the shapes that can be made with the sets of sticks. They *represent* their solutions by drawing the shapes on paper.

The Last Word

COMMENTS FROM TEACHERS ABOUT GEOMETRY

LOOKING BACK

What Activities Can I Change?

◆ The children enjoyed the Shape Step activity and played it like a hopscotch game, jumping from one triangle to another and hopping over those shapes that weren't triangles.

◆ I found another way to do the Mystery Sticks activity. Rather than use clay to connect the ends, I used pipe cleaners and fed them through the straws. Children then connected the sides by twisting the pipe cleaners together.

How Did My Students Surprise Me?

◆ After enjoying the Where's the Bunny? activity, the children decided to make a map to the playground from our classroom. They tried to remember where certain landmarks were, and we recorded them. I was amazed at what they remembered and the sequence of the directions they gave. I was so excited to see that one of my students remembered that "the stairs were next" on the map. He impressed us all!

◆ My three-year-old class liked the [quilting] activity! One little girl said, when the activity was finished, "It looks like my momma's quilt, 'cept it's not made of cloth. It's paper!"

LOOKING AROUND

What Else Could I Do?

◆ The Where's the Bunny? activity gave me so many more ideas. The children wanted to reread the book and get a new map every day to find a new "treasure." They also wanted to make maps for their classmates. I have decided that we are going to make maps every week or they are going to read one every week. The vocabulary they used was fantastic, and it can only get better!

Have You Thought About?

◆ I am going to laminate the pages for the "block-stacking game." This activity may be one of the best prekindergarten games ever. It allowed every child to be an active participant and learner. The "Yes" and the "Oh, well!" comments helped everyone feel the despair of a falling stack, as well as the excitement of a high stack. I loved it, and so did my children!

LOOKING FORWARD

How Will I Change My Practice?

◆ I am going to stop just telling children about three-dimensional shapes and, instead, provide many experiences for them. The Lots and Lots of Boxes activity gave me some new ideas.

◆ I am going to start challenging my children more. I thought the Triangle Blocks activity was too hard for my kindergartners. Initially, most of them were frustrated by trying to fit the triangles into the square blocks. When I acknowledged that the task was difficult, they kept working. Then children began to fit the triangles together. They were so proud and started helping each other. The finished quilt turned out great, and everyone kept bragging about it. What a rewarding experience!

Chapter 4
Algebra

THE BIG PICTURE

SELECTED EXPECTATIONS FROM *Principles and Standards for School Mathematics*

In prekindergarten through grade 2, all students should–

- sort, classify, and order objects by size, number, and other properties;

- recognize, describe, and extend patterns, such as sequences of sounds and shapes or simple numeric patterns, and translate from one representation to another;

- analyze the ways in which both repeating and growing patterns are generated;

- illustrate general principles and properties of operations, such as commutativity, using specific numbers;

- model situations that involve the addition and subtraction of whole numbers, using objects, pictures, and symbols;

- describe qualitative change, such as a student's growing taller; and

- describe quantitative change, such as a student's growing two inches in one year. (NCTM 2000, p. 90)

YOUNG CHILDREN'S MATHEMATICAL THINKING ABOUT ALGEBRA

When children learn about patterns, they are beginning to think algebraically. They see patterns in clothing, wallpaper, and picture books; they hear patterns in words, stories, and music; and they recognize patterns as they proceed through their daily activities. Identifying patterns helps children make sense of their world and accurately predict events yet to occur. Children are naturally interested in patterns, and preschool teachers and parents can take advantage of this interest by helping children recognize, copy, and extend both repeating patterns and growing patterns.

Identifying Patterns

Recognizing and copying patterns are important ways in which children learn. They learn to speak, in part, by copying the sounds that other people make. They learn to write, use utensils and other tools, and play by watching what others do, then repeating what they have seen. Before age five, children can learn to copy simple patterns made with objects and, subsequently, can learn to extend and create their own patterns (Clements 2004). Some adults are surprised to learn

that kindergarten children can also determine the *core unit* of a repeating pattern, such as AAB in the pattern AABAABAABAAB…, and can use this ability to determine that two perceptually different patterns, such as AABAABAABAAB and ✳✳∧✳✳∧✳✳∧✳✳∧, actually have the same structure. Further, young children can hear the auditory patterns in counting beyond 20, that is, 21, 22, 23, 24, 25, and so on, and can see the visual patterns in numerals on a hundreds chart.

Describing Change

Change is a part of every young child's world. Children describe the changes they see with words, for example, when a child says, "When I was little, I couldn't drink out of a cup," or with quantitative ideas, for instance, "When the car ramp was up high, my car went two blocks farther than before." Such descriptions of changes also indicate that children are beginning to think algebraically.

ALGEBRA ACTIVITIES

The following chart provides a brief description of each activity in the next sections.

NAME OF ACTIVITY	DESCRIPTION	PAGE
Lulu the Llama Helps Hanny Learn to Make Patterns	Children create movement patterns in conjunction with Lulu the Llama's strange sounds.	91
Time Capsule	Children describe changes in their lives by illustrating pages for a book and creating time capsules that will be opened at the end of the year	95
Pattern Count	Children use physical patterns to count verbally.	98
Patterns with Pairs!	Children recognize and extend number patterns when they investigate things that come in twos.	100
Mrs. McTats and Her Houseful of Cats	Children act out a story that contains a growing pattern, then represent the story physically and visually.	103
Writing Music	Children represent patterns as they write music to perform in a "rock concert."	106

Lulu the Llama Helps Hanny Learn to Make Patterns

Bring out the Honey Bear stick puppet, and enact the following scenario.

Hanny the Honey Bear: Oh, what fun it is to visit the zoo! I wonder what big animal I will meet next? Wait… I hear a jingle, jangle; jingle, jangle sound. I wonder what it could be? I turn to look at the top of a nearby fence and see an animal peeking over at me. She has two long ears sticking straight up; two big, brown eyes; and a long, soft, white, furry neck with something tied around it.

Next bring out the Llama stick puppet.

Lulu the Llama: Hello, hello, hello! Am I big enough for you? I am five feet tall, and my name is Lulu the Llama. I'm originally from South America, just like you, but I didn't live in the rain forest. I lived on a ranch, which was a lot like this zoo. When I lived on the ranch, I had a special job: I watched over a flock of sheep to keep them safe.

When I heard all the commotion the baby elephants were making, I woke right up out of a sound sleep. From what I heard, you seemed to be having lots of fun. Do you want to come over and play with me now?

Hanny the Honey Bear: I do want to play with Lulu. I climb up the fence and scamper to the top. Holding my tail upright for balance, I run along the top of the fence and stand right next to Lulu. I ask Lulu about that interesting sound she just made and where it comes from. She nuzzles me and sniffs at me in a friendly way.

Lulu the Llama: Can you guess where the sound comes from? It comes from the bells around my neck. I am the only animal in the zoo that has bells! Don't they make pretty sounds?

Hanny the Honey Bear: Lulu gives me a big grin and starts to run all around her paddock, shaking her head back and forth to make sure that I can hear her bells go "jingle, jangle; jingle, jangle." Lulu shakes her head over and over to ring her bells as hard as she can: "jingle, jangle; jingle, jangle; jingle, jangle; jingle, jangle."

Lulu the Llama: Here is my mathematical puzzle for you: What pattern does the sound of my bells make?

Hanny the Honey Bear: Lulu's bells make the sounds "jingle, jangle; jingle, jangle; jingle, jangle; jingle, jangle." I think I am going to need some help from my friends. Can you help me figure out what the pattern is?

Teacher: [to the class] Can you make the sounds that Lulu's bells make? [The teacher writes this sound pattern on chart paper, using a different-color pen for each of the two sound words to show the pattern to the children who cannot read words.] What part of the sound pattern is repeated as Lulu rings her bells?

Circle each *pattern unit,* or repeating part—in this instance, "jingle, jangle," on the chart paper for the children.

Lulu the Llama: You did a great job figuring out the sound pattern of my bells! All that hard work makes me hungry! I think it is time to eat some hay.

Hanny the Honey Bear: I watch Lulu as she walks over to her pile of hay and starts chewing. I hear the sounds "chomp, chomp, munch." She looks up at me mischievously as she eats.

Lulu the Llama: I just made another pattern for you. Can you figure it out? Here is my next mathematical puzzle: What pattern does the sound of my mouth make when I eat?

Hanny the Honey Bear: While she eats, Lulu's mouth moves up and down, and I hear, "chomp, chomp, munch; chomp, chomp, munch; chomp, chomp, munch."

Teacher: Can you make the sounds that Lulu's mouth makes? What is the sound pattern that is repeated as she eats her food?

At this point, write the sound pattern on the chart paper, using a different-color pen for each of the two sound words.

Hanny the Honey Bear: When she eats her favorite food, I notice Lulu's tail moving back and forth, and I hear, "flick, flick, flick, swoosh; flick, flick, flick, swoosh." There it goes again: "flick, flick, flick, swoosh; flick, flick, flick, swoosh."

Teacher: Let's make the sound that Lulu's tail makes. What is the sound pattern that is repeated as she swishes her tail?

Write this sound pattern on the chart paper, using a different-color pen for each of the two sound words, then have one of the children come up and circle each of the pattern units on the chart paper. The children may notice how the pattern grows with the different sounds, that is, AB, AB; AAB, AAB; AAAB, AAAB.

Lulu the Llama: You know, when I grew up on the ranch, the children liked to make movements to go with the sound patterns that I make. Do you think your friends would like to play that game?

Hanny the Honey Bear: I'm sure they would, Lulu. It sounds like fun.

CONDUCTING THE ACTIVITY

Goals: Recognize, describe, and extend patterns, such as sequences of sounds and shapes or simple numeric patterns, and translate them from one representation to another

Suggested Context: During a lesson

Groupings: Whole group, small group, or one adult and one child

Recommended Age Range: 4–5 years

Materials: Hanny the Honey Bear and Lulu the Llama stick puppets (templates for animal stick puppets are found in appendix C); chart paper on which to write Lulu's sound patterns; two markers of different colors, one for each sound in the patterns

Description

1. Ask the children to create patterns of physical movements to accompany the sound patterns for Lulu's actions.

2. Show them an example for the "jingle" and "jangle" sounds. Plan a movement to go with each sound, such as arms out to go with "jingle" and arms down to go with "jangle."

3. As a group, practice making both the physical and sound patterns for "jingle, jangle; jingle, jangle." Continue until all children are capable of reproducing the sound pattern with the accompanying physical movements.

4. Next, break the children into groups, and have each group select physical movements to go with the two other groups of sounds that Lulu makes: (1) her mouth sounds, that is, "chomp and munch," and (2) her tail sounds, that is, "flick and swoosh."

5. Have each group combine the individual movements and sounds to make up pattern units of sound and movement.

6. After the children finish creating and practicing their sound-movement patterns, have them come together as a whole group and ask the small groups to share their new sound-movement patterns.

7. As a whole group, have the children decide which movement they want to make with each sound. Practice these sound-movement patterns together as a group.

Expectations

Some children may have trouble identifying the different patterns. These children may have an easier time discovering the sound patterns when they are written on the chart paper in different colors. Translating the sound patterns to movement patterns is another way to engage children in discovering the different patterns.

> Translating sound patterns to movement patterns is another way to engage children in discovering different patterns.

◆ The concept of the *pattern unit* may be difficult for some children to understand. If you think that children do not understand this term, simply refer to the pattern unit as the part of the pattern that is repeated.

Suggestions for Supporting Learners

Review what the children know about patterns. For example, patterns have parts that are repeated; they are continuous; and they can consist of sounds, movements, colors, shapes, and objects.

◆ Encourage children to find repeating patterns in the classroom or at home.

◆ Have children predict what elements come next in these patterns.

Extensions

Encourage children to think of new sound patterns that might be related to different aspects of Hanny the Honey Bear's adventures.

◆ Encourage children to look and listen for verbal or auditory patterns in their classroom, school, and community. Once sound patterns are identified, children should create physical patterns to represent the auditory patterns.

◆ During circle time, have children create physical patterns that involve standing and sitting for each of the three sound patterns. For example, start by repeating the pattern "jingle, jangle." Tell the children that you will go around the circle and have them say part of the pattern. If they say "jingle," they will stand; if they say "jangle," they will sit down. Have the children predict what comes next in the pattern, that is, who will sit and who will stand. Try this exercise for each of the sound patterns, and discover the different physical patterns that each sound pattern creates.

◆ Ask parents or caregivers to help children create physical patterns to accompany auditory patterns found in the home, such as the sounds of windshield wipers, the dishwasher, birds, and so on.

Connections

With the world of the child: Patterns exist all around in the child's world, including in songs, everyday routines, colors, and numbers. Encourage children to recognize patterns all around them by discussing existing patterns that are pertinent to their lives.

◆ With other content areas: Patterns exist in nature, for example, in the petals of a flower. Extend your discussion of patterns to science activities, music, poetry, and circle-time discussions of days of the week, months, years, and so on.

> Encourage children to find repeating patterns in the classroom or at home, then to predict what elements come next in these patterns.

Process Standards Addressed: Children *represent* sound patterns using physical movements. They also create their own patterns of physical movement and *communicate* their ideas to their peers.

Source: The lesson was adapted from a patterning activity in *Layla Discovers Secret Patterns* (Casey, Anderson, and Schiro, 2002). This book is one of six storytelling and mathematics adventure books for children in pre-kindergarten through second grade from the 'Round the Rug Math series published by the Wright Group/McGraw-Hill. This material is based on work supported by the National Science Foundation (NSF) under NSF IMD Award No. ESI 97-30698. Any opinions, findings, and conclusions or recommendations expressed in this material are those of the authors and do not necessarily reflect the views of the NSF. The story elements of the following activity have been changed to relate to Hanny the Honey Bear's adventures. However, the camel puppet character in *Layla Discovers Secret Patterns* is related to Lulu the Llama because llamas are part of the camel family and have some of the same personality traits.

CONCLUDING THE STORY

Bring out the Honey Bear and Lulu the Llama stick puppets, and enact a culminating scenario similar to the following.

Lulu the Llama: You created wonderful movement patterns to go with my sound patterns. You and your friends have learned a lot about patterns, Hanny. Now I have a surprise for you. For your next adventure, I am going to take you to meet another animal in the zoo, and I promise, you are going to love meeting him because he looks quite amazing.

Hanny the Honey Bear: Oh, boy! I can't wait!

Time Capsule

Goals: Describe qualitative change, such as a student's growing taller; describe quantitative change, such as a student's growing two inches in one year

Suggested Contexts: At home or in the book-publishing center

Recommended Age Range: 3–5 years

Materials: Container, such as a plastic bag or a box that can be sealed, to hold the time capsule; books about growing up, such as *Now I Am Big* (Miller 1996) or *When I Was Little: A Four-Year-Old's Memoir of Her Youth* (Curtis 1993); poster paper for group recordings; paper for book pages, including one page that has the title "When I Was Young…" and another that has the title "Now I Am 5…"; yarn; crayons

Groupings: Whole group, small group, or one adult and one child

Description

1. Read one of the books describing how a child has grown or changed from when he or she was a baby to the present time.

2. Divide the poster paper into two sections with the headings (1) "When I Was Young …" and (2) Now I Am 5 [or 4 or 3]." List phrases or draw pictures that describe the two time periods in the children's lives.

3. Explain that the children are going to make a class book telling about the differences between when they were young and now that they are older. Introduce children to the book-publishing center, and explain the use of the materials. Have each child draw pictures or write text for two pages, one for the title "When I Was Young …" and one for "Now I Am 5 [or the appropriate age]…."

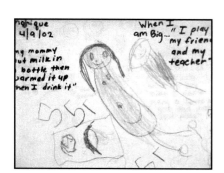

4. When the pages are complete, put the book together and read it as a class. Then state that you wonder how the children will change when they are six or when they go on to the next class. Introduce the idea of a time capsule. Explain that each child will use a bag or a box to hold items that describe or represent her or him at the beginning of the year. The time capsules will then be hidden, and at the end of the year, the same activities will be done again.

5. Children complete the time capsules in small groups. The items to be put in the boxes or bags will vary depending on the age of the children. Some suggestions are a yarn piece that shows how tall the child is, a picture showing all the people and pets in the child's family, a card that shows the child's name written in his or her best handwriting, a tracing of the child's footprint, a handprint made in paint or traced, and a photograph of the child's best smile, with or without teeth. Remember to put the children's names on their bags or boxes.

6. Celebrate the hiding of the time capsules.

7. At the end of the year, do all the activities again and open the time capsules to see how the children have changed.

Expectations

◆ Children will believe that they are currently old and will have many exciting things to remember about when they were young. In fact, they will have so many things to say that you will probably need an older child or an adult to help with transcribing their thoughts.

◆ Children will remember that the time capsule is hidden and may ask you repeatedly when it can be opened. A calendar placed by the hiding place can serve as a reference for those who need it.

Suggestions for Supporting Learners

◆ If children have a difficult time describing changes, encourage them to tell about the change with words rather than numbers. Give them suggestions using terms that are related to mathematics, such as *taller, stronger, longer, older,* and so on.

- If children have a difficult time measuring their heights, show them how to place one end of the yarn on the floor and stand on it while their partners measure their height.

- Continually use "change" vocabulary to talk about differences in the classroom, for example, "We have five more gerbils now" or "Our lunch line is longer because we have more students in our class." These observations will enable children to describe the changes that have occurred in themselves when they open their time capsules at the end of the year.

- This activity can be especially positive for children who have special needs. Select time-capsule ideas that involve skills or processes on which the children will work all year. At the end of the year, they will be proud when they describe their changes, and everyone can celebrate!

Extensions

- Time capsules can be opened in the middle of the year, and changes can be recorded on paper. At the end of the year, children will be able to talk about the first change and the second change.

- Plant growth, the weight of a pet, or the number of jumping jacks that a child can do are all examples of measures that change and can be described. Children can use words and numbers to describe and record the changes that occur.

- Time capsules might contain many additional items, including those that children suggest. Some items or ideas could be represented by children on sheets of paper, which could then be placed in the time capsule.

Connections

- With the world of the child: Change is a part of every child's world. Mathematical expressions that use words or numbers give children vocabulary to talk about changes in their environments.

- With other mathematics: Measuring change often involves number and measurement concepts.

- With other content areas: Writing pages for class books is a wonderful classroom activity that relates to language arts, reading, and the visual arts.

Process Standards Addressed: Children *communicate* as they describe changes and *represent* those changes as pictures for their books.

Sources: *When I Was Little: A Four-Year-Old's Memoir of Her Youth,* by Jamie Lee Curtis (New York: Scholastic, 1993).

Now I Am Big, by Margaret Miller (New York: Greenwillow Books, 1996).

> Change is a part of every child's world. Mathematical expressions that use words or numbers give children vocabulary to talk about changes in their environments.

Pattern Count

> These activities offer practice in rote counting only, that is, in simply learning the verbal sequence of the numbers. The skill of counting also includes keeping track of what has been counted and understanding one-to-one correspondence.

Goals: Recognize, describe, and extend patterns, such as sequences of sounds and shapes or simple numeric patterns, and translate them from one representation to another

Suggested Contexts: During transition time or outdoors

Recommended Age Range: 4–5 years

Materials: One set of number cards, enough to make a hundreds chart

Groupings: Whole group, small groups, or one adult and one child

Description

1. The following activities highlight three counting methods that help children recognize the patterns in rote counting:

    ◆ "Body count"—Children learn a sequence of five body motions to use as they count: (1) raise hands over head, (2) touch the top of the head, (3) touch shoulders, (4) touch waist, (5) touch knees. The same sequence is repeated as children count to twenty-five or more. After children have learned the sequence, they repeat it, whispering all the numbers, then saying out loud the numbers they say when they touch their knees. The written numbers that are said out loud can be found on the hundreds chart.

    ◆ "Roll and clap"—Children sit and count by slapping their legs as they say each number, except for any numeral that ends in the digit 5 or the digit 0. When a numeral ends in the digit 5, children roll their hands. When a numeral ends in the digit 0, they roll and clap their hands. The actions for the multiples of 5 and 10 take longer to complete. The written "roll" numbers and "clap" numbers can be found on the hundreds chart.

    ◆ "Dance it!"—Children select two motions to perform as they count, one motion for the even numbers and the other for the odd numbers. On a hundreds chart, if the even numbers are colored red and the odd numbers, blue, children can see the pattern and "dance it" more easily.

2. After children have mastered these pattern counts, ask one child to point to the numbers spoken on the hundreds chart. For example, in "body count," a child can point to the number that is spoken out loud. In "roll and clap," a child can point to the number that receives a roll and a clap. In "dance it!," the child can point to the number that has either the even or the odd motion.

Expectations

◆ At the beginning of the three counting activities, you will not hear much oral counting. Children will have to concentrate on learning the physical motions before they can perform the motions and count at the same time.

◆ Some children will not match their counting with the physical motions. With practice, most children will come to understand the idea of one-to-one correspondence and will match one motion to one count.

◆ Even after children have experience with these activities, you will notice that they say some of the early "teen" numbers quietly (eleven, twelve, thirteen, fifteen). Because the spoken names for these numbers do not follow a pattern, children need a good deal of practice before they can successfully say the numbers while performing the physical motions.

◆ After practice, children will begin to remember the physical patterns better than you do. They will correct you when you lose count and be able to help you "do it right!"

◆ Children will begin using these counting sequences to count objects or actions on their own. Often, you will observe them as they perform the actions or emphasize particular numbers while counting out loud.

Suggestions for Supporting Learners

◆ These activities help children connect one number word with one action. Although they are rote-counting activities, they also emphasize the idea of one-to-one correspondence, which is necessary for correct counting.

◆ If children have difficulty counting using the corresponding physical motions, repeat the motions slowly and more frequently.

◆ Ensure that all counting activities are modeled, both physically and orally, by a counting leader, either a child or a teacher.

◆ The names for 11, 12, and 13 are especially difficult for children because they do not follow a verbal pattern. Displaying the written numerals while the children are counting out loud is important because the written forms do follow a pattern.

Extensions

◆ Children can place the numerals on the hundreds chart as the counts continue. Shouted numerals or those for which children roll or clap their hands can be colored in some way to show that they are special.

◆ Children can verbalize the patterns they see in these special numerals.

◆ Children can design their own number-pattern "dances."

Connections

◆ With the world of the child: Counting is familiar to young children. They often count as part of their normal play.

◆ With other mathematics: The patterns emphasized in these counting activities are essential to the development of algebraic thinking, as well as understanding of number.

Process Standards Addressed: Children connect the skill of counting with a recognition of the patterns involved in counting.

Patterns with Pairs!

Goals: Analyze the ways in which both repeating and growing patterns are generated

Suggested Contexts: At home, in the art center, as a table activity, or outdoors

Recommended Age Range: 3–5 years

Materials: Toys, household items, clothing, finger paint or washable tempera paint, magazines and catalogs

Groupings: One adult and one child or a small group

Description

> Hearing an adult read "two pairs of woolly socks" from One Snowy Night, *the four-year-old child interrupts to ask, "What is a pair?" The adult replies, "A pair is two things…you know, a pair of socks has a sock for each foot, or two socks. When the book says, 'two pairs of woolly socks,' it means that the boy put on four socks, two on each foot."*

1. Use common items, such as socks, gloves, mittens, or shoes, to explore a pattern of pairs with a child. Organizing a toy closet and sorting laundry are everyday contexts in which pairs are created. Describe patterns of pairs out loud; for example, "I have one pair of shoes, two pairs of

shoes, three pairs of shoes...." Next determine how many items make each part of the pattern, and state the numeric pattern; that is, "Two shoes are in one pair, four shoes are in two pairs, six shoes are in three pairs...."

As an adult and a child cleared off the shelf of the hall closet, they found one pair of gloves, two pairs of mittens, and three pairs of socks. The adult says, "One pair is two gloves. How many mittens are in two pairs?"

> *The child counts, "One, two, three, four—four mittens."*
> *The adult asks, "And how many socks in three pairs?"*
> *The child replies, "One, two, three, four, five, six—six socks. Hey, it's like two, four, six."*

As a three-year-old child dresses Barbie dolls, many pairs of miniature shoes and boots are at Barbie's feet. An adult unconsciously fumbles with the shoes and begins to organize them into groups—one pair of hiking boots, two pairs of knee-high boots, three pairs of sandals, and four pairs of heeled pumps— counting, "Two, four, six, eight; that's twenty shoes in all."

---

2. At the painting center or outside on a sunny day, have children create a book, *Patterns of Pairs: Hands and Feet.* Pour some tempera or finger paint into a foam tray. With adult guidance, children press the palms of their hands or the bottoms of their feet into the paint, then onto paper. After each child has made his or her handprints or footprints and the papers have dried, the prints can be cut out and pasted on several pages to make a book. Page 1 will have one pair of handprints, or two hands; page 2 will have two pairs of handprints, or four hands; and so on. The rest of the pages will follow the same pattern until all the children's handprints are used. The book can then be placed in the class library.

3. Have children make shoe books that contain catalog or magazine pictures of pairs of shoes. The shoe pairs can be cut out and pasted on the individual pages in patterns, such as one pair of shoes, or two shoes; two pairs of shoes, or four shoes; three pairs of shoes, or six shoes; and so on.

Expectations

◆ Most children are aware of things that come in twos, but many may not be familiar with the term *pair*.

◆ Most children are able to memorize the sequence 2, 4, 6, 8 from constant repetition, but they will need to be reminded of the *pair* idea frequently.

Suggestions for Supporting Learners

◆ Make a game of finding things that come in twos. A good introduction to this game is to start with body parts, such as two eyes, two hands, and two legs. Listen for words that describe things that come in twos, such as *twins, bicycle,* or *partners.*

◆ To focus on pattern pairs, use number as the defining part of the pattern, such as one pair, two pairs, three pairs, and so on.

Extensions

◆ Perform pair-patterning activities with repeating patterns, as well as the growing pattern of number. For example, line up a pair of blue socks, then a pair of red socks, then a pair of blue socks, and so on. Children can then describe the repeating pattern of color, as well as the growing pattern of number.

◆ Use a die that has only pair numbers on it, for example, one that reads "2, 2, 4, 4, 6, 6," and invite children to play a familiar board game.

◆ Use plastic animals, or have children pretend to be animals to role-play a Noah's ark scenario. Have children track the number of animals on the ark after each pair comes on board, that is, two at first, then four, then six, and so on.

Connections

◆ With other mathematics: Patterning is an essential concept in mathematics. Number sequences, such as 2, 4, 6, set the stage for more formal work with multiples and multiplication.

◆ With other content areas: Children's books often involve pairs or illustrate patterning sequences in story form. The counting sequence, that is, the pattern of adding one more, is commonly found in many books, poems, and songs. Oral language and listening skills are promoted by such rhymes as "One, Two, Buckle My Shoe" and other songs and poems.

Process Standards Addressed: Children create and *represent* growing patterns with handprints, pictures, and toys.

> Patterning is an essential concept in mathematics. Number sequences set the stage for more formal work with multiples and multiplication.

Mrs. McTats and Her Houseful of Cats

Goals: Analyze the ways in which both repeating and growing patterns are generated; use objects, pictures, and symbols to model situations that involve the addition and subtraction of whole numbers

Suggested Contexts: As a theater or table activity

Recommended Age Range: 4–5 years

Materials: Counters; paper and crayons; *Mrs. McTats and Her Houseful of Cats* (Capucilli 2001; alternative selections include *Counting Crocodiles* [Sierra 1997], *Hippos Go Berserk!* [Boynton 1996], or any other books that use growing patterns in the story); cat faces made from paper plates; apron or some other prop for Mrs. McTats; art paper; fifteen colored dots per child

Groupings: Whole group, small group, or one adult and one child

Description

1. Show the cover of the book. Ask children whether they are good at pretending. Explain that they are going to act out the story of *Mrs. McTats and Her Houseful of Cats*. Talk about the picture on the front of the book, and ask for a volunteer to be Mrs. McTats. Dress Mrs. McTats in an apron, and have him or her come to the front and sit in a rocking chair.

2. Begin reading the story. When you get to the phrase "She lived all alone except for one cat" (p. 1), ask children what else is needed to act out the story. Select one "cat," and give him or her a paper-plate cat face. Ask children to provide the four legs for each cat as it enters the story.

3. Continue reading. As each cat is added, new actors will join the play until everyone in the class is part of the story. Ask children to add sound effects throughout the story, such as meowing when Mrs. McTats goes to the market or purring when she returns with food.

4. After the story is over, ask all the children to pretend that they are Mrs. McTats. Distribute paper, and have children draw pictures of their houses.

> The act of pretending is important for young children's beginning use of symbols to represent objects or ideas, a skill that can be difficult for some children to master.

> The questions and phrases you choose to highlight from the story depend on the book you are reading. For example, for *Counting Crocodiles*, children can draw the island and the water, and the counters can be used to represent crocodiles.

5. Next distribute counters to each child. Explain that you are going to read the story again and that they should place counters on their house drawings to match the number of cats in the story. Tell the children to pretend that the counters are cats. Ask, "Do you think you can pretend?"

6. Begin reading the story as children model your actions and answer the questions in the text. For example, the story reads, "In walked two cats. Was there room for two more?" (p. 3) Watch to make sure that the children add two more counters to their house pictures.

7. Use the words in the text to check children's understanding. For example, the phrase "I only had one cat, but now I have…[three]" (p. 5) could be used to check children's understanding of the number of cats that are now represented on their pictures.

8. As the pattern continues in the book, ask children to predict how many cats will enter the house each time Mrs. McTats opens the door.

9. Count how many cats are in the house at the end of the story. Review the events of the story by modeling them again on your house picture or work mat. Ask children to tell you what would happen next if the story went on and on. Ask how they know.

10. Have children choose partners; while one partner tells the story, the other adds counters to the house work mat.

11. When the partner work is completed, distribute fifteen colored dots to each child and ask the children to make pictures showing the number of cats they have in their houses with Mrs. McTats. The dots can represent the cat faces, and children can add the ears, body, and tails.

Expectations

◆ Some children will add an incorrect number of counters to their mats when you say "two more came." Rather than add two more counters, they will add one to make a total of two. Model the correct addition on your mat, or add the two counters to the child's mat as you say, "two *more*."

◆ Some children will be able to predict what comes next easily. For those children, skip several pages in the story and ask what they think will happen.

Suggestions for Supporting Learners

◆ For children who have difficulty visualizing the meaning of *two more* or adding to make a *total of three,* continue using as many physical representations of the problem as possible. Use new stories or other characters, or have children line up using a +1, +2, +3 pattern.

◆ For children who have difficulty representing the problem symbolically with pictures, ask them to draw one cat immediately after they take one counter off the page. They should continue making their drawings in the same way until their houses are finished and all the cats are included.

Connections

◆ With the world of the child: Two of these stories are familiar to children. Although the crocodile story is unrealistic, the fantasy is certainly one that children enjoy. Further, children often want many pets in their homes or want to invite more friends to a party than their parents will allow. They can relate to the idea of too many people or animals under one roof.

◆ With other mathematics: This activity involves children's understanding of number and operations.

◆ With other content areas: Translating words into actions is an important part of understanding text. This activity allows children to use literature to conduct a mathematical investigation and predict what will happen next, another objective that is important in reading.

Process Standards Addressed: Children *solve problems* by answering the question "How many cats now?" throughout the story. They also *represent* the problem physically in dramatization and on their work mats, as well as pictorially when they make their own drawings.

Sources: *Hippos Go Berserk!* by Saundra Boynton (New York: Simon & Schuster, 1996).

Mrs. McTats and Her Houseful of Cats, by Alyssa Satin Capucilli (New York: Margaret K. McElderry Books, 2001).

Counting Crocodiles, by Judy Sierra (Orlando, Fla.: Harcourt Brace & Co., 1997).

> If you are reading *Hippos go Berserk!*, children can draw the inside of the house decorated for the party, and the counters can represent hippos.

> Regardless of the book you read to the class, you can still use such phrases as "Add one more, Add two more, Add three more," "How many do you have now?" or "What do you think will happen next?" All these ideas are important in growing patterns.

Writing Music

Goals: Recognize, describe, and extend patterns, such as sequences of sounds; translate from one representation to another

Suggested Context: Music center

Recommended Age Range: 4–5 years

Materials: Music paper, two colors of adhesive dots or plain dot stickers that children can color themselves, costume materials, plastic visors, pipe cleaners, ribbons, paste, scissors, construction paper, other scrap paper

Groupings: Small group or one adult and one child

Description

Day 1

1. Gather children in a group, and begin to create a simple repeating pattern using claps and foot stomps, for example, "clap, stomp, clap, stomp…." Ask children to copy your pattern and extend it at least ten times.

2. Ask children to show another way they can make a sound with their hands, feet, or mouths, for example, tapping the tops of their heads or making a "bop" sound with their mouths. With children's help, create a different repeating pattern using their sounds.

3. Repeat the second step using different sounds, a different pattern, or a combination of both.

4. Tell children that their sounds remind you of music. Comment that you would like to remember the "musical" patterns they have just created. Ask for suggestions about how you could remember the pattern if you wanted to re-create it later. Ask children to select their favorite pattern.

5. Show children the music paper, and ask them to re-create one of their favorite "musical" patterns using colored dots, one color for each action, on the paper. For example, if the repeated pattern is "stomp, tap, tap," it could be recorded on the music paper with a red dot, blue dot, blue dot. The familiar song "B-I-N-G-O" has a two-part rhythm that can also be recorded on music paper: B (clap), I (clap), NGO (snap, snap, snap).

6. When the music paper is filled with dots, explain that the song is over.

7. Ask children to "read" the newly written music by replaying it slowly as you point to each dot. Write the composers' names on the music paper.

8. Distribute dots and music paper, and ask children to write their own musical patterns.

9. Play the patterns created by asking the composer to tell the other children what they should do for each dot. Ask composers to point to each dot as children "play" the music. Each composer should sign his or her composition.

Day 2

1. Provide materials in the music center for costumes for "rock bands." Ask children to make costumes that have repeating or growing patterns.

2. Plan a time for a "rock concert" when children can play their songs while dressed in their pattern costumes.

Expectations

◆ Children may create rather sophisticated visual patterns.

◆ Children may write many "musical compositions." These creations can easily be added to a class book in the music center.

◆ Children may create music by using a position pattern. For example, they may place one dot on one line and the next dot on a line below.

◆ Some children may want to place dots on particular instruments. Then, when the child sees the red dot on the music, he or she plays that instrument.

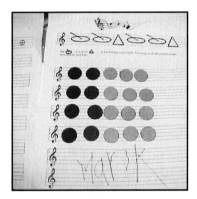

Suggestions for Supporting Learners

◆ As you represent children's created music, tell the children that they must slow the pattern down so that you can "remember" and "write" the pattern with dots. This statement will support the child who does not see the purpose of recording the pattern or does not associate one dot with one action.

◆ Similarly, when the group reads another child's music, ask children to read the pattern slowly while they perform the action represented by the dot. Again, this exercise should emphasize the idea of one dot for one action.

◆ For children who are having difficulty with the idea of dots as a representation of the pattern, ask them to simply create a pattern with dots. After they have created a visual pattern, help them name the action for each dot.

◆ Provide some ideas for costumes that use patterns, such as stripes or polka dots.

◆ For children who have hearing impairments, allow them to "feel" the music by tapping the pattern on their hands. Some children may be able to feel music by placing their hands on a speaker.

Extensions

◆ Children may quickly tire of the sounds modeled at the beginning of the lesson. For variety, they can use instruments that they have created in the music center or, perhaps, use newly invented sounds.

◆ Have children create additional visual patterns and representations by—

- representing two actions performed at the same time with two overlapping dots,
- placing dots directly on the instruments that are to be played, or
- making marks around the dots to show that certain actions are drawn out for "long" playing.

◆ Children's music can be placed in a class book in the music center where others can read and play it.

Connections

◆ With the world of the child: Music is an important part of a child's world. Teachers might display examples of musical scores for favorite songs and lead a discussion of similarities and differences among pieces of music.

◆ With other mathematics: The patterns created by children may be spatially oriented, offering a direct connection with the Geometry Standard (NCTM 2000). The dots can be placed "up and down" on the music paper, and the music can be read by children using those words. Children can also play their instruments or clap their hands "high and low," and the music can be read by children using those words.

◆ With other content areas: The activity of reading music using dots is directly related to reading letter symbols. Likewise, writing music using dots is directly related to writing letters to spell out children's names.

Process Standards Addressed: Children *represent* musical patterns using colored dots. They then use musical sounds to *communicate* their patterns.

Children represent musical patterns using colored dots, then use musical sounds to communicate their patterns.

The Last Word

COMMENTS FROM TEACHERS ABOUT ALGEBRA

LOOKING BACK

Where are my students now?

◆ The children in my class are good at recognizing two- or three-step linear, repeating patterns.

What activities can I change?

◆ I realized that children need time to "see" counting patterns. First, they are very interested in counting; then, they love to do the physical patterns. Putting them both together takes time.

How did my students surprise me?

◆ They continually see patterns all around them. They tell me about patterns on the bathroom floor, the cafeteria, my clothing, the wallpaper—everywhere!

◆ I was absolutely amazed by the way my children performed the rock concert and enjoyed writing music. They had so much fun putting it together, writing the music, then "conducting" the presentation. The colored dots appeared on their instruments and on many pages of music. They held their instruments up high when the dot was high on the music paper and low when the dot was low. Later, when members from the symphony came to perform, the children wanted to see their music and were eager to show the symphony conductor their "compositions." The whole experience was exciting.

LOOKING AROUND

Have you thought about…?

◆ I am a parent. I knew my child did patterns at school, but I never knew they were important for algebra! I had never thought about it until I tried some of these lessons. I am going to start emphasizing this more at home.

How can I showcase…?

◆ There are patterns all over my classroom! I have never spent much time looking for them, but my children are finding them for me. The rug, the curtains, the way the dishes are organized on the shelves, and the book labels are all examples of different patterns.

LOOKING FORWARD

Where are we going?

◆ I never would have realized that the time-capsule activity was part of algebra. Children love to talk about how they have grown or what they have learned to do. The objective for this activity is easy to [r]each and one that I can see is a beginning of "algebra math."

What should I start doing?

◆ I realized that I have never thought about or taught growing patterns in my prekindergarten class. I also realized that many of the songs we sing and the movements we make are examples of growing patterns. My children are doing them. I just need to tell them!

Chapter 5
Measurement

THE BIG PICTURE

SELECTED EXPECTATIONS FROM *Principles and Standards for School Mathematics*

> **In prekindergarten through grade 2, all students should—**
>
> - recognize the attributes of length, volume, weight, area, and time;
> - compare and order objects according to these attributes;
> - understand how to measure using nonstandard and standard units;
> - select an appropriate unit and tool for the attribute being measured;
> - measure with multiple copies of units of the same size, such as paper clips laid end to end; …
> - use tools to measure. (NCTM 2000, p. 102)

YOUNG CHILDREN'S MATHEMATICAL THINKING ABOUT MEASUREMENT

Measurement involves assigning a number to an attribute of an object, such as the length of a pencil or the capacity of a jar. Young children know that these attributes exist, but they do not know how to reason about them or measure them accurately. Preschool children are interested in measuring and begin to develop important measurement concepts from the ages of three to five (Clements 2003). This chapter addresses the following components of measurement:

- ◆ Attributes, units, and processes
- ◆ Techniques and tools

Attributes, Units, and Processes

Children's initial ideas about the size or quantity of an object are based on perception. They judge that one object is bigger than another because it looks bigger. For example, given two balls of clay that are identical, with one rolled into a hot-dog shape, the preschool child will usually say that the hot-dog shape has more clay (Piaget and Inhelder 1967). Given two pieces of string of equal length placed side by side on the floor, with one formed to make a loop, a young child may say that the extended string is longer.

Five-year-olds can learn significant ideas about measuring. They can arrange objects side by side to compare their lengths. They can compare two objects of significantly different weights by holding one in each hand to feel the difference in weight. They can also place a smaller leaf on top of a larger one to see which has the greater area, provided that the smaller leaf fits within the boundary of the larger leaf.

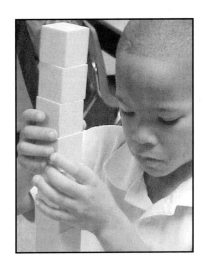

Five-year-olds can begin to learn the process of measuring with nonstandard units. They can lay identical pencils or pieces of chalk end to end beside a broom to measure the length of the broom. They can cover a sheet of paper with sticky notes to measure the area of the sheet of paper. The significant difference between measuring with units and measuring by comparing is that measuring with units yields a numerical result, such as that the broom is seven pencils long.

Techniques and Tools

Measuring requires specific techniques, skills, and concepts that children develop throughout their school years. Older research held that children should progress in a rigid sequence: first measuring with nonstandard units, such as pencils; then measuring with standard units, such as centimeters and feet; and finally, measuring with rulers. Current studies suggest that children can benefit from using rulers along with concrete models of units, even during beginning activities with measurement (Clements 2003). As children gain more experience, they learn that they cannot allow gaps or overlaps between the concrete units used to measure length, that one must start at 0 when using a ruler, and that the unit lengths on a ruler, rather than the marks above each number, must be counted.

Children in the preschool years develop many important measurement ideas that can be extended in subsequent schooling. Teachers should remember that measurement activities with preschoolers are exploratory; mastery is not yet the goal.

MEASUREMENT ACTIVITIES

The following table provides a brief description of each activity in the next sections.

NAME OF ACTIVITY	DESCRIPTION	PAGE
Hanny Learns about Measuring from Morty, the Long-Legged Moose	Children answer Morty's questions about the sizes of animals in the zoo. Comparative vocabulary is emphasized.	113
Measure March	Children act out specific directions to demonstrate their understanding of measurement vocabulary.	117
Guess How Much I Love You	Children measure and compare a variety of lengths, just as Little Hare does in the story *Guess How Much I Love You*.	119
What Is Taller?	Children use the words *taller* and *shorter* to compare the heights and lengths of objects.	121
Footprints	Children analyze footprints to determine the sizes of the people who made them.	124
How Long Is a Minute?	Children predict activities that take "longer than a minute" or "less than a minute."	126

Hanny Learns about Measuring from Morty, the Long-Legged Moose

STAGING THE SCENARIO

Bring out the honey-bear and llama stick puppets (templates are found in appendix C), and enact the following scenario.

Lulu the Llama: Hanny, I promised to show you a wonderful animal, and I have a mathematical riddle about this animal for you to solve. Are you ready? First, walk along the fence with me over to the next yard.

Hanny the Honey Bear: Lulu takes me over to the other side of the fence and sticks her nose over it. I am looking at the strangest animal I have ever seen! Who is this amazing creature, Lulu?

Lulu the Llama: Listen to my riddle, and you will find out:

Teacher: [Brings out the Moose stick puppet]

I have someone to introduce.
This is Morty, the Long-Legged Moose.

Now, close your eyes and try to be wise.
Is he short? Is he tall? What is his size?

When you look from the side,
His long nose can't hide,

But when you look him in the face,
It is as wide as outer space.

His antlers stand high,
Right up to the sky.

So what do you think?
Is he short? Is he tall?

Just give it a try,
Then tell me why.

Next ask the children to decide whether the moose is short or tall, then to give reasons for their answers.

Morty the Moose: Hello-oo there. Pleased to meet you, Hanny. I come from way up north in Alaska where it gets very cold. Did you know that my front legs are taller than my hind legs so I can jump over fallen trees? I'm glad that you like my beautiful antlers. They grow to be 6 feet wide.

Use a tape measure to show children how wide 6 feet is.

Morty the Moose: I have been alone in this fenced yard, and I am curious about the other animals that live in the world. Maybe you can tell me about them. I have some animal questions that I have been wondering about for a long time.

Hanny the Honey Bear: I'm not sure that I can answer your questions, Morty, because I haven't seen that many animals myself, but I know who can help us (turning to the class). Do you think you could help us?

Next conduct the activity as outlined below.

CONDUCTING THE ACTIVITY

Goals: Compare and order objects according to length attributes; learn how to measure using nonstandard and standard units

Suggested Context: During a teaching lesson

Recommended Age Range: 4–5 years

Materials: Hanny, Lulu, and Morty stick puppets (templates for animal stick puppets are found in appendix C); chart paper with Morty's poem; chart paper with Morty's questions; animal books; six-foot-long "tape measures" (made from string, clothesline, ribbon, tape, or yarn) for each group of children

Preparation Instructions

1. Draw a pair of antlers six feet wide on the chalkboard or chart paper.

2. Write Morty's questions, without answers, on chart paper; use a brightly colored pen for the measurement words, that is, *long, wide,* and *tall.* The questions are as follows:

    ◆ Do you know any long-nosed animals that are not tall? (Answers: alligators, crocodiles, and so on)

    ◆ Do you know any wide-nosed animals that are not tall? (Answers: frog, pig, whale, and the like)

    ◆ Do you know any smaller animals with antlers? (Answer: deer)

    ◆ Do you know any animals that are wide? (Answers: hippo, rhino, and so on)

Groupings: One adult and one child, whole group, or groups of children divided into pairs

Description

1. Read the list of Morty's questions. Use your hands to model the ideas of *wide, long,* and *tall.*

2. Write children's answers on the board. After they have listed as many animals as they can, ask them where they could go to look for other answers to these questions.

3. Distribute animal books, and ask children to find some pictures of animals that could provide more answers to Morty's questions. Add children's questions about animals to Morty's list. Include measurement words in each question.

4. Tell the children that Morty has become interested in learning about their widths. He wants to know whether the children are as wide as his antlers when their arms are outstretched as wide as they can go.

5. Write children's yes-or-no predictions on chart paper.

6. Select one six-foot tape measure, and hold it up to the antler picture on the board. Show how this tool measures the width of Morty's antlers exactly. Explain how the children will know whether their arm spans are as wide as Morty's antlers.

7. Distribute the tape measures to each group. Have the child who is being measured hold one end of the ribbon or string in one hand while another child stretches out the string to the other hand and says, "too short" or "too long."

8. When the children are finished, review their predictions and compare them with the actual results.

9. Children can then compare their "widths" among themselves by directly matching their outstretched arms with the arms of others in the class.

> Direct comparisons are the easiest ones for young children to make.

Expectations

◆ Children may use the words *big* or *bigger* to describe most measurement relationships. They need to learn more specific measurement vocabulary when they are talking about the animals and their comparisons.

◆ The act of measuring from an end point will be new to many young children. Model this procedure throughout the activities, and introduce the idea of a "fair" measurement.

◆ Direct comparisons are the easiest ones for young children to make. They will be able to see whether their arm spans are as wide as Morty's antlers by stretching them out directly on the chalkboard picture.

Suggestions for Supporting Learners

◆ If children have difficulty thinking of answers to Morty's questions, offer several suggestions of ways to begin or model the act of looking for an answer in an animal book. Think aloud as you search.

◆ If children have difficulty deciding whether an animal has a wide nose or is tall, ask if anyone has seen that particular animal before. If children have never seen a certain animal, they will have difficulty using comparative words accurately to describe its measurements.

Extensions

◆ Have one child think of an animal that is tall or small and pretend to be that animal. The other children try to guess the animal, using the words *tall* or *small* and *long* or *short* in their descriptions. If the others cannot guess what animal the first child is pretending to be, she or he will tell them, using the words *tall* or *small* in naming the animal.

◆ Continue to add animal answers to Morty's question chart throughout the subsequent months. Children will be able to identify new animals from video clips, after trips to the zoo, or when they read new books.

◆ Allow children to take the tape measures home and make comparisons with adults, pets, and objects around the house.

Connections

◆ With the world of the child: Children often describe animals and their characteristics. Measurement words are important parts of children's descriptive vocabulary.

◆ With other content areas: This activity can be connected with science as children think about the relative heights, lengths, and widths of different animals.

Process Standards Addressed: Children *solve* Morty's *problem* and *communicate* their solutions to their classmates.

CONCLUDING THE STORY

Next bring out the honey-bear and moose stick puppets and have them enact the following culminating scenario.

Morty the Moose: Can you tell me the answer to my question? When you hold your arms outstretched, are you wider than my antlers?

Point to the chalkboard, and ask the children to tell Morty the answer.

Hanny the Honey Bear: Now you have your answer, Morty. I guess it is time for me to go.

Morty the Moose: Good-bye, Hanny. I wonder who my next visitors will be. Will they be short? Will they be tall?

> The measuring activity can be connected with science as children think about the relative heights, lengths, and widths of different animals.

Measure March

Goals: Recognize the attributes of length, volume, weight, area, and time

Suggested Contexts: During transition times or outside

Recommended Age Range: 3–5 years

Materials: None required

Groupings: One adult and one child, small groups, or large group

Description

1. Children go on a walk. At the direction of the leader, children change how they are walking using their understanding of measurement attribute words.

2. Possible directions for walking are as follows:

    ◆ Walk with long steps.

    ◆ Walk with your arms held high.

    ◆ Walk with short steps.

    ◆ Walk with your arms held low.

    ◆ Walk with fast steps.

    ◆ Walk low on your flat feet.

    ◆ Walk high on your tiptoes.

    ◆ Walk crouched down low.

    ◆ Walk with heavy steps, like an elephant.

    ◆ Walk with light steps, like a mouse.

3. The leader should model the actions as the walk continues.

Expectations

◆ Children enjoy going for walks, but they may forget to listen to the new directions, especially if they are enjoying the previous one.

◆ Children may not understand some of the measurement terms. They will watch for models and copy their actions.

Suggestions for Supporting Learners

◆ Watch for those children who always seem to need a model for their actions. Model with exaggeration to help these children understand your directions.

◆ Vary the order of the directions, and use new measurement vocabulary frequently. All children need practice acting out the vocabulary.

◆ If children have orthopedic impairments, the directions may need to be significantly modified. Create a pathway that ensures that children who depend on wheelchairs and walkers can participate.

Extensions

◆ Do the same activity using instruments from the music center. The leader can give directions for students to march like a marching band. Different vocabulary words can be used to describe the sounds their instruments should make, such as soft, loud, short, long, fast, and slow. If no instruments are available, children can make sounds using two dowel rods with crepe paper streamers attached to the ends.

◆ Distribute animal finger puppets to children, and have them "march" in the same ways that their animals move. Children can then use measurement vocabulary to describe how they are moving.

Connections

◆ With the world of the child: Children love physical movement, and marching is a favorite activity.

◆ With other content areas: Connecting music and physical movement is a familiar practice in early childhood settings. Using measurement vocabulary extends that common practice to mathematics.

Process Standards Addressed: Children listen and respond as measurement vocabulary words are *communicated* to them.

> Using measurement vocabulary extends the connection between music and physical movement to mathematics.

Guess How Much I Love You

Goals: Compare and order objects according to the attribute of length; understand how to measure using nonstandard and standard units.

Suggested Context: During story time

Recommended Age Range: 3–5 years

Materials: *Guess How Much I Love You* (McBratney 1994), two colors of yarn, scissors

Groupings: One adult and one child or one older child with a younger child

Description

1. Read *Guess How Much I Love You* with a child. Point out how Little Hare shows how much he loves other characters by stretching his arms as far as they can go. Help the child cut a yarn length that shows how far his or her arms can stretch. Ask the child to help you cut the length of yarn that shows how far you can stretch. Stretch out the two yarn pieces, and ask the child to compare to see which one is longer and which one is shorter.

2. Cut more lengths of yarn to show how high the child can reach, how long his or her stride is, and how far he or she can jump.

3. End the activity by letting the child pick a final measurement. If the child chooses a distance that cannot be measured with yarn, such as "to the moon and back," ask her or him to think of something that can be measured.

4. Send the yarn measurements to someone the child loves with the accompanying verse from the book. This activity may be especially appropriate during the week of Valentine's Day.

Expectations

◆ Children will enjoy the book and may tell you that they play a similar game at home or at grandma's house.

◆ Children may want to change the starting point for their measurements to show that their lengths of yarn are longer than those of their adult partner.

◆ Children may measure with the yarn, then make an incorrect observation about measurement, such as "I jumped 6 pounds" or "I am five!" Realize that children often do not know the words to describe measurement. Do not disagree; in response, state ideas about measurement using correct comparison terms, for example, "Your yarn is longer than your hand" or "You jumped farther than I did."

Suggestions for Supporting Learners

◆ Children love to show how far they can stretch, jump, or step, but they do not always know "fair" ways to compare lengths. Before comparing the yarn lengths, have children make a direct comparison between how far they can stretch their hands and how far an adult can stretch his or her hands.

◆ Stretching the string to the appropriate length may be difficult for children. Continue to emphasize the idea that the measurement must be fair, and model the act of starting at the beginning point and cutting the yarn at the ending point to show a "careful" measurement.

◆ If children want to know the distance they jumped or stretched, show them the yarn. If they still have questions, let them use other measuring equipment to help them understand these lengths.

Extensions

◆ Children can use their lengths of yarn to measure objects in a room or to encircle their waists or wrists. Encourage them to use comparison words to describe measurements that are longer, shorter, or taller or require more yarn, less yarn, or about the same lengths of yarn.

◆ Children can take their yarn pieces home and compare them with lengths created by their older siblings or parents.

Connections

◆ With the world of the child: This activity is focused on the world of the child. Children constantly compare themselves with others using measurement terms. "I am taller," "My dad is bigger than your dad," or "I can jump more than you!" are all familiar statements in a young child's world.

◆ With other content areas: This story presents many beautiful images for the young reader, and the mathematics flows naturally from the story. Further, the measurement concepts taught in this lesson directly relate to those taught in science.

Process Standards Addressed: Children *solve the problem* of comparing by directly *representing* two measurements with lengths of yarn and developing the ability to *reason*.

Source: *Guess How Much I Love You,* by Sam McBratney (Cambridge, Mass.: Candlewick Press, 1994).

What Is Taller?

Goals: Recognize the attributes of length, volume, weight, area, and time; compare and order objects according to these attributes

Suggested Contexts: At home, during transitions, outside, at centers

Recommended Age Range: 3–5 years

Materials: Objects in children's immediate surroundings, including people, toys and blocks, household items, food products, furniture, trees and shrubs, large boulders, and monuments

Groupings: One adult and one child or small groups

Description

> When a child asked for a big glass of milk, an adult placed two glasses on the table in front of her and asked her to choose the bigger one. When the child indicated the taller glass, the adult slowly moved the smaller glass toward the taller one, touching the tall glass about two-thirds of the way up its length, and said, "You want the taller glass today."

> Objects that share the same surface have a common baseline from which to compare height.

1. When two people or objects share a common surface and are close to each other, ask children, "Which is taller?" For example, people usually stand on the floor, glasses or cups sit on the table, and picture frames rest near each other on the shelf. After a child makes a choice, move the shorter object toward the taller one and state which is taller. Repeat similar comparisons with a variety of everyday items, sometimes asking, "Which is shorter?"

> Just before using a new toothbrush, a child points to the thin, long handle section near the bristles and states, "Look, Dad, my new one is like yours." Then, the child places both toothbrushes on the vanity and continues, "But mine is shorter." The adult leans closer to the toothbrushes and agrees: "So it is."

2. Place two objects flat on a surface, and ask a child, "Which is shorter?" For example, a knife and a fork are placed on a napkin, two favorite dolls are held in a hand, and two books lay next to each other on the coffee table. Ask the child, "How do you know which is shorter?" or "Why do you think so?" To check the answer, stand each of the objects side by side on a flat surface so that they touch. With the child, look closely at the tops of the two objects to see whether one is above the other or whether they are in line. State what you notice: "Look, the fork and knife are the same height" or "Your book is taller than mine."

> Holding two miniature flags in his hand with both top points level, a young boy exclaimed, "They're the same at the points!" He then made a side-by-side hand motion to check to see whether the tops were indeed in the same position. A few seconds later, he rests the bottoms of the flag posts on the table and states, "But if I put them down like this, this one is taller." The adult and the child look at the flags together as the adult confirms, "This one is taller. We were tricked because the bottoms were hidden in your hand."

When children first explore the concept of measuring height, they are not always aware that the items need a common baseline.

Expectations

◆ Some children insist that two objects whose heights differ slightly are the same. This idea is reinforced by the children's uneven hand movements in making a comparison. Most children have more success in making comparisons when the objects chosen are markedly different in height.

◆ When children are first exploring the concept of measuring height, they are not always aware that the items need a common baseline. Some children choose to line up the tops of the objects and compare the opposite ends. Others line up the tops and forget the bottoms. Many will choose a surface as a baseline and compare the tops.

Suggestions for Supporting Learners

◆ When comparing the heights of two objects, say what you notice out loud and actively show and tell children how you made your decision.

◆ Be consistent with the language you use in your responses and requests. In this comparison of heights, *taller* and *shorter* are more appropriate adjectives than *bigger* or *higher*. The terms *higher* and *lower* should be used when you are describing the location of an object, such as, "We can put your teddy bear on a higher shelf than your cars." When used appropriately, *bigger* usually refers to a multidimensional comparison in which one object may be taller, wider, and heavier than another. To use the word *bigger* when focusing on one dimension, such as height, can be misleading.

◆ Ask questions that help children focus on their actions and assumptions. For example, "Are you sure this one is taller? Why do you think so? If I place the two glasses on the table, is your glass still taller than mine?" Be sure to ask, "Which is shorter?" just as often.

◆ If the objects being compared are not aligned, help children line up the top or bottom of each object. Usually, objects are lined up by resting the bottoms on a common surface and observing the tops. Of course, keeping the tops level and looking at the bottoms for a comparison is also appropriate.

Extensions

◆ Go on a scavenger hunt. Choose one object, and look for other objects that are shorter than the selection. Both adults and children should tell one another what objects they found and explain how they made decisions about the objects' heights.

◆ Compare objects that are segmented. After a child has built a tower with blocks or boxes, ask her or him to build a shorter tower; or build two towers with the child's help, then ask which is shorter or taller. If blocks of the same size are used in each tower, count the number of units, that is, blocks, to justify the comparison instead of using a hand gesture. In other words, you might comment, "This tower is taller because it has two more blocks."

Connections

◆ With the world of the child: Children love to explore their environments. Height is easily observed as young children look at tall bookcases, skyscrapers, or tree branches.

◆ With other mathematics: When children sort toys or objects, they may do so by comparing height. When children make graphs, the importance of a common baseline is emphasized.

◆ With other content areas: Children's literature is a wonderful context in which to explore size concepts, such as height, in both text and illustrations. Science activities, such as measuring plant growth, require height comparisons.

Process Standards Addressed: Children *communicate* the language of mathematics as they use the words *taller* and *shorter* to describe their observations.

> When children make graphs, the importance of a common baseline is emphasized.

Footprints

Goals: Compare and order objects according to length attributes

Suggested Context: As a table activity

Recommended Age Range: 4–5 years

Materials: Footprints picture and "Big Feet, Little Feet" activity sheet (see photographs on the following page)

Groupings: Small group with one adult

Description

1. Make one enlarged copy of the footprint picture for the class and one copy of the "Big Feet, Little Feet" activity sheet for each child.

2. Show children the picture of the footprints. Engage them in a discussion of the illustration by asking such questions as the following:

   ◆ What do you see? (Footprints)

   ◆ How do you know that they are feet? (They have five toes.)

   ◆ How many people made them? (Two)

   ◆ How can you tell? (The picture shows two big feet, a right and a left, and two little feet, a right and a left.)

   ◆ Where do you think they are walking? (On a beach, on wet sand, on wet concrete)

   ◆ How did you decide? (Answers will vary; most likely, children will cite their own experiences.)

3. Engage children in a discussion of the relationship between the size of the feet and the number of footprints. Ask questions similar to the following:

   ◆ Do you see more small footprints or more big footprints? (More small footprints)

   ◆ Why do you think you see more small footprints in the picture? (Children may answer, "You can fit more small ones in" or "The big ones take more room.")

4. Give each child a copy of the "Big Feet, Little Feet" activity sheet and crayons. Have children draw pictures of the people who made the footprints.

5. Engage children in a discussion of their completed pictures. Ask them to tell you about the person who has big feet and the one who has little feet.

6. Collect the pictures, and place them where all children in the group can view them. Point out all the pictures of people who have big feet, and ask children to tell you about their similarities and differences. Do the same for the pictures of people with little feet. Next ask children to tell you how the people with big feet are different from the people with little feet.

Expectations

◆ To determine that the picture shows more small footprints than big footprints, each child will want to count and compare the numbers of footprints, despite the fact that the greater number of small footprints is easily seen without counting. Allow each child to count to verify the numbers. Have children identify the greater number after each count.

◆ When identifying similarities and differences among drawings of the people who made the footprints of each size, children usually identify age, height, and gender attributes. For example, they may say that the big footprints were made by an older person, a tall person, or a man. Similarly, they may say that the small footprints were made by a child, a short person, or a girl. Some children will keep gender the same and differentiate by age, saying that the big feet belong to a "mommy" and the small feet belong to a little girl.

Suggestions for Supporting Learners

◆ Although children may not know the vocabulary to describe the relationship between the size of the footprint and the number of footprints, they will realize that the picture shows fewer footprints when the footprints are larger. Encourage children to describe the relationship in their own words.

◆ Some children may have difficulty drawing the people that they can visualize in their minds. Some may wish to label their drawings with identifiers, such as *boy, girl, man, lady, dad, mom,* or *kid,* to help other children pick out the similarities and differences among people with big feet and those with small feet. If children want to label their drawings, assist them in doing so.

Extensions

◆ In the comparisons of drawings, some children will say that older people have bigger feet than younger people do or that men have bigger feet than women. To explore these ideas, invite adults and young people, males and females, to visit your class. Have children compare the foot sizes of the visitors.

◆ To provide more experience with the relationship between the size of a unit and the number of units, have children walk across the room by taking giant steps and counting their steps. Record the number of giant steps for each child. Ask, "If you take baby steps across the room, how many baby steps do you think you will take? Do you think that you will take more baby steps than giant steps? How did you decide?" Have children check their predictions by taking baby steps across the room, counting the steps, and comparing their results with their predictions and with the number of giant steps they took.

Connections

◆ With other mathematics: In this activity, children not only explore measurement ideas but also use concepts of number. They count to compare number of footprints. They count their own baby and giant steps. They also use numerals to represent those quantities.

◆ With other content areas: Children make drawings to illustrate their ideas. They write words and phrases to describe their drawings. They use oral communication to describe their observations and the mathematical relationships they see.

Process Standards Addressed: Children *communicate* their *problem solutions* in this activity. They *represent* their *reasoning* by drawing pictures of the people who made the footprints.

Source: Big Math for Little Kids, by Herbert Ginsburg, Carole Greenes, and Robert Balfanz (Lebanon, Ind.: Dale Seymour Publications, 2003). The tasks in this section are modified from the activity "Footprints" in this source.

How Long Is a Minute?

Goals: Recognize the attributes of length, volume, weight, area, and time; compare and order objects according to these attributes

Suggested Contexts: During story time and throughout the day

Recommended Age Range: 4–5 years

Materials: A one-minute sand timer or another timer that shows when a minute of time has elapsed; chart paper; pictures or photographs of different activities, such as a student writing his name, the class walking to the cafeteria, children during rest time, the class playing outside, the class eating lunch, a student getting a drink of water, a child snapping her fingers, a child opening a door, and so on; the book *Tikki Tikki Tembo* as retold by Arlene Mosel (New York: H. Holt & Co., 1989)

Groupings: Whole group or small groups

Description

1. Read the story *Tikki Tikki Tembo*.

2. Discuss the problem presented in the story. Extend the discussion to include why one brother's name took so long to say and why the other brother's name did not.

3. Ask students whether they have ever heard the word *minute*. Ask them to explain when they heard it, who said it, and in what context it was used.

4. After this discussion, explain to students that you have a tool that shows just how long a minute lasts. Show them the one-minute sand timer, and tell them that when the top container of sand empties into the bottom container, one minute has passed. Turn the timer over two or three times, allowing the sand to run out each time, to help students visualize the passing of a minute. Ask children to close their eyes, then open them when they think a minute has passed. Talk about their estimates.

5. Challenge students to think of some things that they can do that would take longer than a minute, such as the activities shown in the photographs. Write these responses on chart paper below a space entitled "Activities that last longer than a minute." Generate a similar list for events that last less time than a minute.

6. Throughout the day, test the students' predictions by measuring their suggestions with the sand timer.

7. Verify the results by placing a longer or shorter clothespin on the photographs of the activities tested. When all the activities have been tested, compare the results with the students' predictions.

8. On the basis of their findings, ask the students to predict how long other activities not mentioned would take, using the sand timer as a reference.

> Many students will have different understandings of how long a minute lasts.

Expectations

◆ Some students will not understand the importance of starting the timer exactly when the event being measured begins.

◆ Many students will have different understandings of how long a minute lasts. Almost all children have been told to "wait a minute" by their parents and have then experienced a span of time that seems to be much longer or much shorter than a minute, depending on what they were waiting for and what they did while they were waiting.

Suggestions for Supporting Learners

◆ Every time an activity is performed and tested, display the sand timer for students to see. Doing so will give them a frame of reference to use in measuring the event and comparing it with other activities. You might also appoint a student to watch the timer and tell everyone when all the sand has run from one side to the other.

◆ Remind students that the sand timer must start exactly when the event being measured starts so that the event can be measured accurately. Demonstrate the importance of this action by starting the timer after the class begins a particular activity. Discuss whether this way of measuring was fair or unfair, allowing students the opportunity to establish a standardized signal at which to start the timer.

Extensions

◆ List the events measured in this lesson in order from those that last longest to those that last shortest. Have students begin two or three different activities at the same time; children can then easily see which activity is finished first.

◆ After the class has had many opportunities to measure events using the one-minute sand timer, allow students to estimate how long events may last using a three-minute timer.

◆ Allow students to sign out the sand timer for use at home. Encourage parents to perform various activities with their children to discover how long the events will last.

◆ Create a class book of drawings from students of the events they tested that lasted about a minute. Title the book *Things That Last about a Minute.*

Connections

◆ With the world of the child: Young children are not able to abstract the meaning of elapsed time as displayed on a clock, but they are aware of what a clock is and are curious about the time it shows. Relating a vocabulary word, such as *minute*, to activities and routines that children experience from day to day allows them to connect mathematics with their world.

◆ With other mathematics: The sequencing of routine events can be used as an illustration of patterns in the environment. Children use their knowledge of when events happen during the day to predict what activity will come next.

◆ With other content areas: Children need to understand sequences of events to follow and create story structures. Understanding the beginning, middle, and end of a story is essential for developing comprehension strategies in reading.

Process Standards Addressed: Children *solve problems* and *reason* to make predictions about events and to learn how the time expired during an event relates to a minute.

Source: Tikki Tikki Tembo, by Arlene Mosel (New York: H. Holt & Co., 1989).

> Young children are aware of what a clock is and are curious about the time it shows.

The Last Word

COMMENTS FROM TEACHERS ABOUT MEASUREMENT

LOOKING BACK

What activities can I change?

◆ My children enjoyed making lots of measurements for the Guess How Much I Love You activity. We measured our heads, our arms, our shoes, how far we could stretch, and so on. When we were finished, they put all their measurements in [plastic bags] labeled with their names, made heart cards, and took their measurements of love home!

How did my students surprise me?

◆ My students thought of their own ways to march in the Measure March activity and were able to use measurement vocabulary to describe their new "walks." They added, "crawl slowly, like a caterpillar"; "walk with a tall neck, like a giraffe"; and "take wide steps, like Morty the Moose." The story saga fit nicely here.

◆ Children's responses to the Footprint activity surprised me. Some children not only drew pictures showing people with big and small feet, but they also began measuring distances with big steps and small steps. When asked why the numbers of steps were different, they responded, "It takes more small prints to get where the big prints go." "The small is more because the big takes up more space." My most surprising response was from a little boy who said, "Isn't it weird... the big feet are a little number and the small feet are a big number...."

LOOKING AROUND

Where else can I find this content in the immediate environment?

◆ As a parent, I had never thought about doing measurement comparisons throughout the day. The What Is Taller? activity gave me lots of ideas.

LOOKING FORWARD

Where do we go from here?

◆ I am going to spend much more time on math. I found that my children were very interested in these activities, and every one I tried could have been a two-day lesson or even more!

How will I change my practice?

◆ I will use much more measuring vocabulary. My child often says, "bigger than…," and now I am saying, "Do you mean 'longer'? 'Wider'? 'Heavier'?"

◆ After doing the Minute activity, I am going to stop using exact minute expressions. Instead, I am going to say, "about one minute," "more than one minute," or "less than one minute."

Chapter 6
Data Analysis

THE BIG PICTURE

SELECTED EXPECTATIONS FROM
Principles and Standards for School Mathematics

> **In prekindergarten through grade 2, all students should—**
>
> - pose questions and gather data about themselves and their surroundings;
> - sort and classify objects according to their attributes and organize data about the objects;
> - represent data using concrete objects, pictures, and graphs;
> - describe parts of the data and the set of data as a whole to determine what the data show. (NCTM 2000, p. 108)

YOUNG CHILDREN'S MATHEMATICAL THINKING ABOUT DATA ANALYSIS

Data analysis is the process of classifying, organizing, representing, and using information to ask and answer questions. This topic is relatively new to the elementary mathematics curriculum but involves important mathematics and is of great interest to children. Data analysis enables children to ask and answer such questions as "What is the favorite flavor of ice cream in our class?" "What is the favorite sport?" and "How many letters are in our first names?" Classifying data is a necessary skill in data analysis. Initially children sort before they count the number of items in each group. Later they are able to count the number of items in a group as they sort them. For example, when sorting color tiles, initially a child will put all the red ones together, then the blue ones, and so forth, before counting the number in each category. Later, the child can count all the blue tiles as he or she sorts them, then repeat this process for the other colors (Clements 2004).

Another developmental aspect of data analysis is the ability to use categories (Russell 1991). For example, children may make a list of others in the class, then record each child's response to a question beside his or her name. Later children learn to classify these responses into categories.

Given that children normally progress in their representation of information from concrete to pictorial to symbolic, their data representations should progress in the same way. Initially they may use physical objects, such as shoes, to make graphs; later they may use pictures of objects, such as photos or drawings of shoes; and finally, they may use symbols for shoes, such as *B* for brown shoes and *W* for white shoes (Friel, Curcio, and Bright 2001).

Data analysis is fun for, and appealing to, children when it relates directly to their lives. Teachers can take advantage of that appeal by structuring data analysis activities with children's interests in mind.

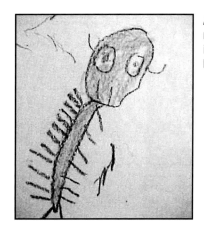

A four-year-old's representation of an insect he found in the Buried Treasure activity

DATA ANALYSIS ACTIVITIES

The following table provides a brief description of each activity in the next sections.

NAME OF ACTIVITY	DESCRIPTION	PAGE
Help Hanny Make a Graph about Your Favorite Zoo Animals	Children create a pictograph to show Hanny their favorite zoo animals.	132
Toys of All Sorts!	Children sort toys and explain the reasoning being their groupings.	136
Buried Treasure	Children find buried treasures, represent their findings, and describe the objects' attributes out loud.	139
My Missing Sock	Children describe their socks, using attributes and reasoning to find matches.	141
Creature Caves	Children reason to identify the hidden attribute of creatures in a cave.	144
Polling the Crowd	Children pose questions and record responses using a bar graph.	147

Help Hanny Make a Graph about Your Favorite Zoo Animals

STAGING THE SCENARIO

Bring out the Honey Bear stick puppet (see template in Appendix C), and enact a scenario similar to the one that follows.

Hanny the Honey Bear: Hello, children, it's Hanny the Honey Bear once again. The sun is beginning to come up over the big zoo, and all the sleeping animals are waking up. I guess I should go home to the children's zoo. I carefully and silently slip through the window, scamper back to my cage, pull the door shut, and click the lock into place. All is quiet and peaceful in the children's zoo. I'd like to take a nap, but when I close my eyes, my mind is full of the new and exciting animals I met on my adventure tonight.

[Next bring out the prairie dog, baby elephant, llama, and moose stick puppets. Have different children hold the puppets as Hanny names them.]

Hanny the Honey Bear: Before I go, I would like your help in figuring out one last puzzle. I have been thinking and thinking, but I just can't decide which of the animals that we met on this adventure is my favorite. Can you tell me what animals we have met? Yes, we met Yippy the Prairie Dog; Binky, Boo, Bobo, Baba, Beany, and Bart, the baby elephants; Lulu the Llama, and Morty, the Long-Legged Moose. Here is my question: What kind of animal was your favorite? [Pause] I would like to know this information about everyone in your class. Can you collect the data and find out which kind of animal your class liked the best? You can make a graph to help me see how many children liked Yippy the best, how many liked the baby elephants the best, and so on. Then, when I'm sitting in my cage at night with nothing to do, I can remember our wonderful adventure together and look at your great graph to figure out all kinds of interesting information.

CONDUCTING THE ACTIVITY

Goals: Sort and classify objects according to their attributes, and organize data about the objects; pose questions, and gather data about the group and the classroom environment

Suggested Contexts: During the teaching of a lesson

Recommended Age Range: 4–5 years

Materials: All animal puppets (see templates in appendix C), 3-by-5-inch index cards, butcher paper

Groupings: Small groups or large group

Description

1. Pose the first problem to the children: How can we figure out who likes which type of animal the best?

2. Bring out the stick puppets. Talk about possible methods for solving the problem. Remind children that Hanny wants something she can see when she wakes up, something that will remind her of the answer to the problem when the children are not available to help her.

3. Encourage children to come up with a variety of solutions for sorting their choices. Suggestions may include lining up in groups, drawing pictures of their favorite animals and displaying them on butcher paper, raising their hands to vote, or holding up animal cards.

4. Have the whole group choose and carry out a plan for sorting.

5. After the children have chosen their favorite animals, remind them that they must now count how many children liked each animal the best. Tell them that Hanny would like to keep a record of this information, and ask them how they can make such a record. Children can attempt to make their own graphs or recordings.

6. Display and discuss the various ways that the children made their recordings. Talk about good ideas or challenges that appear in each of the recordings.

7. Introduce the idea of a pictograph as another way of making a record for Hanny.

8. Distribute an index card to each child. Ask children to draw pictures of their favorite animals and to label their pictures with the appropriate words. Provide help as needed.

9. Then, using the chart paper, sort the pictures so that all like animals are in a row, making a pictograph or bar-graph model. Decide as a class how to label the graph. Remind children that Hanny will want to know the names of the pictures in each column, as well as the title and authors of the graph.

10. Count the cards in each column together, and ask children which animal is the class favorite. Ask children whether they can tell which animal was chosen as the favorite without counting. Discuss the way of comparing that is suggested.

11. Have children talk about what they discovered in the graph to tell Hanny the Honey Bear. You might ask some of the following questions:

    ◆ Is the number of children who preferred Yippy the Prairie Dog more or fewer than the number of children who preferred the baby elephants? Is the number of children who preferred the baby elephants more or fewer than the number of children who preferred Lulu the Llama?

    ◆ Which two animals did most children prefer?

    ◆ How can we find out how many students did not prefer Morty the Moose?

    ◆ What else can we tell Hanny about the graph?

Expectations

◆ Some children may want to choose more than one animal.

◆ Some children may have difficulty choosing a method to count the number of children who prefer each animal. Encourage the class to share answers and ideas.

◆ Children typically have difficulty coming up with their own way of recording "how many." Allow them to collect their own data, create their own recording charts, and use their own ideas. Then, when the activity becomes too frustrating or confusing, introduce the pictograph method and discuss any previous problems that developed.

> Allow children to collect their own data, create their own recording charts, and use their own ideas.

Suggestions for Supporting Learners

◆ When children appear to be frustrated or confused, acknowledge the fact that solving problems and organizing graphs can be hard. Then offer suggestions for making a graph that Hanny can read.

◆ If children make graphic representations that adequately represent the information Hanny wanted, do not introduce the pictograph. Rather, focus on their representations and discuss the results.

Extensions

◆ Have children come up with their own questions about the class, and work together to sort, collect, and organize information that provides the answers to these questions to send to Hanny the Honey Bear.

◆ The dramatic play area can be reorganized as a zoo. Children can bring toy animals and create areas for each kind of animal. Food supplies, environments, and activities for the animals will need to be planned and organized.

Connections

◆ With other content areas: Collecting and graphing information are important activities in both the science and social studies content areas.

Process Standards Addressed: Children engage in *problem solving* to collect the data, organize the information, and create a graphic representation of a solution for Hanny.

CONCLUDING THE ACTIVITY

Once again, bring out the Honey Bear stick puppet and act out a scenario similar to the following.

Hanny the Honey Bear: Look at the great graph you have made for me. Can you tell me all about what you discovered? [Pause] Now that you have finished answering my question, maybe you can come up with some new questions to answer about yourselves. Then you can collect information about those questions and make new graphs to send to me. I will have lots of interesting math questions to keep me busy when I'm in my cage at night with no one around. And best of all, I'll learn all about you. [Pause] I have learned to solve so many mathematical puzzles with your help. Can you remember each of the different kinds of math puzzles the animals in the big zoo presented to us? Can you tell me about each one we solved? [Pause] Great job; now I will remember all the new math I have learned how to do, and I'll never be bored again! Oh, I hear my nice zookeeper unlocking the door. Good-bye, good-bye; I hope I see you on another night!

> Children engage in problem solving to collect the data, organize the information, and create a graphic representation.

Toys of All Sorts!

Goals: Sort and classify objects according to their attributes, and organize data about the objects

Suggested Contexts: At home, during transition times, at any center

Recommended Age Range: 3–5 years

Materials: Toys, household items, buttons, keys, macaroni, clothing, cutlery, rocks, apples, art materials, and any other materials that can be sorted easily

Groupings: Small groups or one adult and one child

Description

An adult and child are on the floor playing with plastic animals when the child says, "Take the broken ones away."

"OK. Pick the ones that you like, and we will put away the ones that are broken," clarifies the adult.

The child begins to sort the animals: "This one… this one."

Later, the adult says, "You've got some matching cars, don't you? You've got two that look the same. What kind are they?"

The child says, "Tow trucks. But these ones don't look the same."

The adult agrees: "No, here is a black one and another black one, but they are not the same. How many orange cars do you have?"

The child counts, "One, two, three."

To which the adult says, "Three orange cars; how many brown cars do you have?"

The child counts, "Only one, two. Only two."

As the sorting comes to an end, the adult asks, "Where does the orange go if you are putting the cars in color groups?"

A teacher divides her class into small groups to sort keys. The teachers says to one group, "Tell me about your piles of keys."

A child responds: "We made two piles. One pile has keys with teeth on one side, and the other pile has keys with teeth on two sides."

"Which group has the most?" the teachers asks.

In unison, the children respond, "The ones with teeth on one side."

The teacher continues, "What do we know about most keys?"

"They have teeth on one side. They're not like people!"

"What do you mean?" asks the teacher.

"People have teeth on the top and bottom." This answer leads to a discussion of whether any animal has teeth on only one side. The children conclude that animals could not bite if they did not have teeth on both sides.

The teacher then calls on other groups to tell how they sorted their keys. One group sorted the keys by the shape of the head, but some children disagreed. They believed that one particular key did not belong because it "had a bump"; it belonged in a group by itself.

When sorting objects, we initially focus on one attribute and place like objects in a group. The number of groups varies according to the characteristic chosen for sorting. For example, toys may be divided into broken and unbroken sets or into color groups.

1. At home, adults often organize household and personal belongings. In a child's dresser, clothing may be sorted with T-shirts in one drawer, socks and underwear in another, pajamas in a third, and so on. In cupboards, grocery items are sorted with canned goods on one shelf and pastas, rice, and cereals on another. Spoons, knives, and forks are usually sorted in separate cutlery compartments in a drawer. Encourage children to watch and talk about how their parents or other adults sort objects. Have them help sort items in the classroom and add items to already sorted groups.

2. Opportunities for children to talk about, and contribute to, sorting activities often occur during cleanup or setup times in the classroom. Again, children should be encouraged to return items to their proper storage places. Blocks are stored in the block center, cars are returned to the small toy basket, and so on. Children may help set up a writing center by gathering pencils from a pencil cup, paper from a drawer, and picture books from the bookshelf. On occasion, children can help reorganize a center and sort items in different ways.

3. Encourage children to sort their toys and personal objects in their own ways. At home or in a mathematics center, provide children with large sets of objects or collections, such as dolls, vehicles, figurines, buttons, marbles, keys, and so on. Ask them to sort the collections into piles in such a way that all the items in a pile have some attribute in common. Ask children to tell you why they grouped the objects as they did or to take turns guessing why the objects are together.

Expectations

- ◆ Many children sort items into two piles, whereas others are comfortable creating multiple piles. Often, the child chooses some characteristic for sorting, and the number of groups evolves from that choice.

- ◆ Some children may sort toys or objects according to surprising or unanticipated attributes. When observing their sorting behavior, ask questions about the attributes they have selected.

- ◆ Most children initially focus on one attribute at a time when sorting; however, some young children may use more than one attribute or can be supported in doing so. For example, encourage a child to sort red shirts and red pants, blue shirts and blue pants, and so on.

Suggestions for Supporting Learners

- ◆ If children have difficulty sorting by one rule, separate the objects into a *yes* pile and a *no* pile. For example, hold one item up and ask, "Is this red?" If the answer is "yes," then it goes in the yes pile. If not, the object is placed in the no pile. When all the items are sorted, ask the child to show you all the red objects, then all the objects that are not red.

- ◆ Encourage children to sort and to assist in sorting a variety of objects to make sure that some items "are not in the wrong place." Asking children to help find lost or miscategorized objects is often a way to involve them in natural sorting.

Extensions

- ◆ Provide less familiar objects, or suggest less familiar attributes, such as texture, for children to consider in the sorting activity.

- ◆ Use magazine pictures to play sorting games, and record results by gluing or taping pictures to a larger piece of paper.

- ◆ Encourage children to be "detectives" and guess how you or some of their peers sorted a set of objects.

Connections

- ◆ With the world of the child: Visiting stores and performing routine chores are opportunities that expose children to sorting arrangements in their day-to-day activities.

- ◆ With other content areas: Social studies, science, and language all require classification and sorting skills. Making labels for sorted groups is also a part of each content area.

Process Standards Addressed: Children *reason* about and justify their sorting categories. Their reasoning is then *communicated* visually or orally to others.

> Most children initially focus on one attribute at a time when sorting.

Buried Treasure

Goals: Sort and classify objects according to their attributes, and organize data about the objects; represent data using concrete objects, pictures, and graphs

Suggested Contexts: At the sand table or outdoors

Recommended Age Range: 3–5 years

Materials: Sandbox, tubs, or buckets filled halfway with sand or rice; plastic spoons and small paint brushes for the "archaeological" dig; magnifiers; paper; crayons; "treasures," such as small toys, plastic bugs, or any other objects that can be found easily in the sand

Groupings: Small groups or one adult and one child

Description

1. Bury the "goodies" in the sand. Explain to children that they will be archaeologists who are searching for treasure.   Using spoons and small paintbrushes, they will look carefully through the sand to discover the buried treasures.

2. Children search for items and sort them in any ways they wish.

3. Explain that archaeologists must carefully record the objects that they find. Distribute paper, and show children how to fold a sheet into two or four sections. Ask children to record the objects they have found by drawing pictures and grouping items that are the same on the same section of the paper.

4. When the recordings are finished, they can be displayed on the bulletin board and discussed in small groups. For example, one child might say that his favorite treasures were silvery, and the other children in the group could point to any treasures they found that were also silvery. Further, the teacher might state a "not" attribute, such as not blue, and children could identify treasures they found that were also not blue.

Expectations

◆ Children will want to investigate the objects carefully if you emphasize the role of the archaeologist.

◆ Children will represent found objects in unique and often surprising ways. Emphasize that recording the results accurately is important, but expect some added details. Children's imaginations often create new, unseen attributes, which will be represented in some of their pictures.

> Children's imaginations often create new, unseen attributes, which will be represented in some of their pictures.

◆ Children's schemes for categorizing objects in certain sections on their papers may not be obvious to you. Ask them to tell why particular objects are next to others, but do not be surprised if children cannot verbalize their reasoning.

Suggestions for Supporting Learners

◆ If children have difficulty representing the objects they find, ask them specific questions, such as "What color is it?" "How many dots are on it?" "Do you see a pattern?" "How can you draw the bumps on this object?" "Do you have enough " _____ ?" and "How many _____ do you need to make your picture look just like the object you found?"

◆ If children have difficulty representing their treasures in the folded sections of the paper, ask them to record only their two favorite treasures. Then their pictures can be used for the group discussion later.

◆ If children sort and represent their treasures easily, ask them to give you a word that describes all their objects, then ask them to tell how each object is different from the others.

Extensions

◆ Sort small objects in the room in large bins by color, shape, or material, and label each bin with a picture and name.

◆ Ask children to repeat the activity. This time, their papers should be folded in fourths. One representation should be placed in each section. Then, after the representations have been made, the sheets can be cut into fourths and a large pictograph can be made to show what the children found. Two categories could be used. In one category, the treasures would have a specific attribute, and in the other category, the treasures would not have the specific attribute.

Connections

◆ With the world of the child: Data are represented in a variety of forms in the environment of children. For example, blocks in the block center are placed on labeled shelves and categorized by type, attendance or snack charts are used to tell who is present or who is in charge of bringing snacks, and clothes are placed in particular drawers classified by type.

◆ With other content areas: Although the purposes are different, representations of data are frequently necessary in both science and art activities.

Process Standards Addressed: Children *represent* their treasures and *communicate* the results of their "dig" by telling about their pictures.

> Children's schemes for categorizing objects may not be obvious to you.

My Missing Sock

Goals: Pose questions and gather data about the group and the environment; describe specific items of data and the set as a whole to determine what the data show

Suggested Contexts: During a teaching lesson, during story time, or at home

Recommended Age Range: 3–5 years

Materials: *A Pair of Socks* (Murphy 1996); one paper bag for each student, labeled with his or her name; chart paper; real pairs of socks that are different from one another but have some similarities. Ask parents to send in pairs of socks that are old, outgrown, or no longer used; other pairs can be purchased in thrift shops.

Groupings: Small groups or one adult and one child

Description

1. Read *A Pair of Socks* (Murphy 1996).

2. After reading page 3 of the book, ask students to describe a sock that is missing its match in the story. On chart paper, record the attributes that they describe, such as color, shape, design, size, and so on.

3. Pause each time two socks are compared on a page in the book, and ask students whether the two socks are a correct match. Have students justify their responses by explaining how the two socks are alike and different.

4. The final page of the book shows all the socks introduced in the story and their matches. This illustration allows students to find the matching pairs of socks and to identify the attributes that are shown for each match.

5. Show the students a box with pairs of socks that are different but have some similarities. For example, all socks might have white backgrounds or stripes of some kind.

6. Make sure that the number of children matches the number of socks and that each sock has a match to ensure that pairs of children will have matching socks.

7. Have each child pull one sock out of the box without showing it to anyone and hide it in the bag labeled with his or her name.

8. Tell the children that they are to find their matching socks. Explain that each child will use words to describe the sock hidden in his or her bag while the group listens carefully.

9. As the first child shares a description, others who think that they may have the matching sock stand up. Those students then describe their socks. The rest of the group agrees or disagrees with the standing students and tells why. The socks are then taken out of the bags, and matches are checked.

10. Conclude this activity by asking the class what describing words, that is, *attributes*, helped them know who had the missing socks.

Expectations

◆ Some students may focus on only one attribute instead of visualizing all the attributes mentioned. These students are likely to say that they have a match after hearing only one attribute described.

◆ Some students will need prompting from the teacher to provide more information about their socks.

◆ Some younger students may lack a sufficient vocabulary of attribute words to describe their socks. These students are likely to give only one-word responses, or some of their descriptions may be inaccurate.

Suggestions for Supporting Learners

◆ For students who give only one-word descriptions about their socks, draw a picture of the sock using only the information provided by the child. For example, if a student says that his sock is blue and gives no further clues, try to elicit more information by drawing a blue sock, then asking him whether the picture looks exactly like the sock in his bag. If the student says that the picture does not match his sock, ask, "What is missing?"

◆ Show the students a large sorting board that is divided and labeled into three categories: *yes*, *maybe*, and *no*. Use a happy face as an icon for *yes*, a question mark for *maybe*, and a circle with a line through it for *no*. As each student describes the sock in his or her bag, ask the rest of the students to help sort the possible matches into the appropriate category.

◆ Ask the students how they eliminated some possibilities. For example, why did they eliminate all the red and green socks? The answer might be that the student described her sock as blue.. For students who do not know the names of the colors, provide a color chart that they can use to indicate the colors of their socks.

Extensions

◆ The same procedures for this activity with socks can also be used with other items, such as mittens or buttons.

> Finding similarities and differences among objects with multiple attributes develops young children's observation skills.

◆ Students can play a game to answer the question "Which one of these socks does not belong?" This game can be played with single socks—three that have a like attribute and one that does not, for example, three blue socks and one red sock.

◆ One child can pose questions to the group to find out who has a matching sock. Those who are responding can answer only "yes" or "no."

Connections

◆ With the world of the child: Finding matching sets of clothing is a problem-solving skill that young children practice every day when they dress themselves for school.

◆ With other mathematics: Finding similarities and differences among like objects with multiple attributes develops young children's observation skills for analyzing data and builds the foundation for establishing relationships with variables and functions in algebraic thinking.

◆ With other content areas: When students describe the world around them, they should be encouraged to use their five senses. One of the most important tools in science is the use of the five senses to make observations and predictions.

Process Standards Addressed: Children *communicate* descriptions of their socks to find the correct matches. They identify specific attributes that helped them as they *reason* about whether they were correct.

Source: *A Pair of Socks*, by Stuart J. Murphy (New York: HarperCollins Publishers, 1996).

Creature Caves

Goals: Collect, sort, and organize relevant data to answer a question

Suggested Context: During the teaching of a lesson

Recommended Age Range: 5 years

Materials: Index cards, markers, a large piece of yarn or tape to section off a "cave," and three sets of creature cards, one set each in red, blue, and yellow. (Note that each set has fifteen different blackline creatures created from the templates in Appendix D. Duplicate the cards, and cut them apart to yield forty-five creatures, or about four for each child if you are working in groups of ten children.)

Groupings: Whole class, small groups, or one adult and one child

Description

Day 1

1. Place the creature cards randomly around the classroom floor.

2. Introduce the activity by saying that some friendly creatures have "invaded" the classroom. Ask children to find two different creatures each and bring them back to the large group.

3. When everyone has returned to the group, ask children to look at their creatures carefully and tell their partners about their creatures. Then have children work in groups of six to sort the creatures in any ways they wish. Children may choose from many possible categories, such as hair or no hair; blue, red, or yellow; toes or webbed feet; glasses or no glasses; horns or no horns; smile or frown; and arms or no arms.

4. Observe the classifications, and ask children how they sorted the creatures. Then ask children to sort the creatures in another way.

5. When all the children seem to be finished sorting their creatures, call them together and ask them to explain their classifications to the class. As each classification is identified, write one descriptive word on a card for that grouping; also make one "not" card for each grouping. For example, if a child states that her group has a red creature, use a *red* crayon to write the word *red* on a card. Write red in that color on another card, but place a large black X over the word and say, "not red." Make sure to write the words with as many pictorial clues as necessary to help the children "read" the cards. After you finish writing each card, hold it up and ask the children to hold up a creature card that has the same attribute.

6. Continue this process until you have made at least sixteen cards.

Description

Day 2

1. Before the activity, mark off a "cave" area on the floor of the classroom and distribute two creature cards to each child. Tell children that they will learn a new game with the creatures. Draw one card from the sixteen made the previous day, and ask someone to name the attribute on the card, such as "hair." Show children the cave area, and explain that only creatures that have hair can live in the cave.

2. Children take turns adding their creatures with hair to the cave or placing their creatures that do not have hair outside the cave. When children have demonstrated that they understand the classification system, begin the game.

3. Introduce the game by asking an adult to leave the room with a special "guard." The guard is to make sure that the adult does not hear the group's description. After the adult and guard leave the room, the group selects a secret-word card. That card is hidden somewhere in the room to prevent the adult from seeing it when he or she returns. Everyone in the group knows what the word is and is reminded to keep it a secret from the adult.

4. The adult and the guard return to the room. The adult tries to guess the secret word by asking children whether their creatures belong in the cave. A creature belongs in the cave if it can be described using the secret word.

5. The adult continues to guess creatures until the secret word becomes obvious. The adult should model thinking about the word before guessing it.

6. This game can be played several times in small groups. Always ask the guesser to explain his or her reasoning.

Expectations

◆ Initially, children may sort the creatures randomly and inconsistently. They may explain their groupings by saying, "I like this one" or "These are my favorites." You may not see any consistent rule in their classifications.

◆ Next children may begin sorting creatures using one rule only. They may put all the same-colored creatures or all the creatures with hair together.

◆ Some children may become confused if someone else sorts their creatures using a different rule. Others will easily see that the same creatures can be placed in several categories depending on the characteristics chosen.

◆ Teachers can usually determine that children have reached the level of reasoning required for the game when they are able to sort objects into many different classifications.

> Some children may become confused if someone else sorts their creatures using a different rule. Others will easily see that the same creatures can be placed in several categories depending on the characteristics chosen.

◆ To play the game, children need to see a set of objects that has already been classified, then decide how the objects were sorted. For some children, this task is easy, but for others, it may be difficult. In fact, some children may believe that the adult was able to guess because he or she was "just lucky" or "a good guesser."

Suggestions for Supporting Learners

◆ For children who cannot state an attribute that could be used to describe their creatures, suggest a color and model the sorting with them.

◆ For children who believe that the adult who guesses the secret word is just lucky, play the game frequently. Ask the guesser to think aloud as he or she solves the puzzle.

◆ For children who have difficulty guessing a partner's secret word, let them play the game with the group many more times.

Extensions

◆ Children can play this game as partners, with one child as the guesser and the other classifying the creatures. The game requires a high level of reasoning and addresses the idea of communicating with descriptive language.

◆ Some children will be able to play this game with two caves. Each cave has a different attribute, and children must identify both. In most instances, the attributes for the two caves will overlap, as they might in a Venn diagram.

Connections

◆ With other mathematics: The process skill of reasoning is an essential component of this lesson. Children learn that they can solve problems by thinking, not by guessing or just being lucky.

◆ With other content areas: The descriptive language in this lesson and the use of *not* are important components of language arts and early literacy. For an art center or ongoing center activity, you can also have children make their own caves from boxes and decorate them.

Process Standards Addressed: Children use *reasoning* and *problem-solving* skills to identify the cave attributes. They also *communicate* their answers to the questions of the guesser.

> The caves game requires a high level of reasoning and addresses the idea of communicating with descriptive language.

Polling the Crowd

Goals: Pose questions and gather data about the group and the environment

Suggested Contexts: At home, in a store, at a fair, in school, or in any other location with familiar people

Recommended Age Range: 4–5 years

Materials: Inch grid paper; crayons or a pencil

Groupings: One adult and one child

Description

Five-year-old Aimee and her mother are at a mathematics fair. One booth catches Aimee's attention. The activity encourages older participants to pose a question, gather data from others in the hall, and graph the results on the grid paper provided. Aimee and her mother take a moment to prepare. Aimee's mom asks, "What question do you want to ask some people?"

When Aimee says, "I wonder what people like to draw," her mom writes, "What Do You Like to Draw?" at the top of a piece of paper.

"Let's give them some choices," Aimee's mom suggests. After talking about their preferences, Aimee writes "animals," "flowers," "people," and "houses," all spaced evenly along the vertical line (axis) her mom has drawn for her.

Aimee, with her grid paper and pencil in hand, asks each person she approaches, "What do you like to draw: animals, people, flowers, or houses?" Either Aimee or her respondent places a check mark in a square aligned with the choice. After asking people of all ages, Aimee looks at the finished graph and exclaims, "Most people like to draw animals, and almost no one likes to draw houses!"

1. Ask a child what he or she would like to know about people at the store, relatives at home, teachers and children in all the kindergarten classes, or children in the neighborhood. Encourage the child to share a question that he or she is interested in asking others. Choose a topic with limited choices that are reasonably obvious, such as "What kind of pet do you have or would you like to have?"

2. Write the question at the top of a piece of graph paper.

3. Write the words or draw pictures to describe the choices at the bottom of the graph paper, one description per square.

4. Discuss an appropriate time for the child to conduct the survey.

5. Have the child ask the question of a variety of people, such as family members, peers, teachers, other parents, and neighbors, and record each response, or ask the respondent to do so, in an appropriate square on the graph.

6. When the graph is finished, discuss the results by asking questions and showing interest in the child's results.

Expectations

◆ A variety of questions will be generated about a variety of interests. Some children may ask questions that require either yes or no answers, such as "Do you like cats?" They may also pose questions that are of interest only to certain groups, such as "What toy do you play with most?" They may pose questions that have multiple answers that are difficult to limit or that span too large a range, such as "What is your age?" Keep in mind that the child should generate the question, but provide assistance to make the process more manageable.

◆ Children may fill in the graph inaccurately. Some children who do not yet appreciate the need for one square to represent one response may color more than one square to represent an answer. Children who make this mistake may also have inadequate motor control to keep their coloring within one square. Others may color more than one response because the respondent liked lots of choices.

Suggestions for Supporting Learners

◆ Some children can easily write or illustrate their own questions on grid paper. Others may need to use stickers to represent the choices, or they may need an adult to serve as scribe for them. A small picture next to each word is helpful when a child surveys other children.

◆ Some children experience difficulty in recording oral responses. Encourage children to ask respondents to point to, mark, or color an appropriate spot for their answers. Asking questions after the graph is completed is important. If a child does not initiate

> Asking questions and gathering answers are important components of data analysis. Children should pose the questions themselves and participate in data collection.

discussion of the findings, then an adult should do so. For young children, focusing on the response with the most squares or the one with no or very few squares is an adequate analysis. For others, you may count the number of squares and discuss which response has the most squares colored.

Extensions

◆ Have children record the data in other ways. Keep a tally of responses, for example, and later, transfer that information to a graph. Have children make a pictograph without grid paper by choosing appropriate stickers and placing them next to their choices.

◆ Use data collected from mixed audiences to make comparative graphs, such as adults' responses compared with children's responses or boys' responses compared with girls' responses. One way to make such a graph is to have different groups use different colors to record their opinions or answers.

Connections

◆ With other mathematics: Data analysis involves measurement and number sense. Children draw conclusions by visually comparing the bars on a graph and learning that the longest or tallest represents the most. Others count the number of squares for each choice and compare numbers to draw conclusions.

◆ With other content areas: Social studies, science, art, and music topics could be used to formulate survey questions. Writing, listening, and speaking are also important in this activity.

Process Standards Addressed: Children create and *represent* the results of a survey question and *communicate* the results to others.

The Last Word

COMMENTS FROM TEACHERS ABOUT DATA ANALYSIS

LOOKING BACK

Where Are My Students Now?

◆ At first, my four-year-old English-language learners had difficulty with "My Missing Sock." Then, when I began pointing to the socks as I said the words and modeling the activity over and over again, they begin to understand it. They enjoyed the suspense of waiting to find out who had their matching socks.

What Activities Can I Change?

◆ I did the "Polling the Crowd" activity on family night at the children's museum. Children needed lots of encouragement at first, but after they asked their first few questions, they became excited.

◆ My children loved the "Buried Treasure" activity! I substituted tongs for the spoons to help their fine-motor skills. Once they completed their "mission," they wanted to start all over. They also loved looking at others' recordings.

How Did My Students Surprise Me?

◆ I tried the Missing Sock activity with my three-year-old class. At first, I thought it was too hard, even though they seemed to enjoy finding socks and using their words to talk about them. Later in the afternoon, one of my students was playing in the rice table, and he ran up to me very excitedly and said, "Look, I found a match! Theses match!" All the while, he was holding up two plates that he found in the rice table that were exact matches to each other. I was delighted that he made the connection between the two activities.

◆ My four-year-olds' recordings of the "Buried Treasure" activity were so detailed that I was amazed! They really felt like they were archaeologists.

◆ I was surprised by the rich vocabulary my four-year-old children used during the Buried Treasure activity. I heard many mathematics terms: "Hey, mine is just like yours!" "Yours is not the same color as mine." "Mine is lots bigger than yours." "I found more than you did." "This one was in the corner of the box."

LOOKING FORWARD

How Will I Change My Practice?

◆ I am going to stop doing all the graphing myself! I used to create all the grids, the squared paper, and the words myself, then children would just color the squares. I never realized that children's graphs could be so good.

How Can I Showcase Data Analysis?

◆ At first, I thought the guessing activity in Creature Caves was too hard for my kindergartners. Our assistant principal guessed red after all the creatures had been sorted, but some of the children still thought that he was just lucky. Since we started school, we have played that game on a regular basis, and most children are getting the idea very well. In fact, they now look at graphs in the hall and try to figure out the rules used in their construction. I think I just need to focus on reasoning more and expect children to do it!

Appendix A

SELECTED EXPECTATIONS FROM *PRINCIPLES AND STANDARDS FOR SCHOOL MATHEMATICS* (NCTM 2000)

NUMBER AND OPERATIONS STANDARD FOR GRADES PRE-K–2
Expectations

In prekindergarten through grade 2, all students should—

- count with understanding and recognize "how many" in sets of objects; …
- develop understanding of the relative position and magnitude of whole numbers and of ordinal and cardinal numbers and their connections;
- develop a sense of whole numbers and represent and use them in flexible ways, including relating, composing, and decomposing numbers;
- connect number words and numerals to the quantities they represent, using various physical models and representations;
- understand and represent commonly used fractions, such as 1/4, 1/3, and 1/2;
- understand various meanings of addition and subtraction of whole numbers and the relationship between the two operations;
- understand the effects of adding and subtracting whole numbers;
- understand situations that entail multiplication and division, such as equal groupings of objects and sharing equally; …
- use a variety of methods and tools to compute, including objects, mental computation, estimation, paper and pencil, and calculators.

ALGEBRA STANDARD FOR GRADES PRE-K–2
Expectations

In prekindergarten through grade 2 all students should—

- sort, classify, and order objects by size, number, and other properties;
- recognize, describe, and extend patterns such as sequences of sounds and shapes or simple numeric patterns and translate from one representation to another;
- analyze how both repeating and growing patterns are generated;
- illustrate general principles and properties of operations, such as commutativity, using specific numbers; …
- model situations that involve the addition and subtraction of whole numbers, using objects, pictures, and symbols;
- describe qualitative change, such as a student's growing taller;
- describe quantitative change, such as a student's growing two inches in one year.

GEOMETRY STANDARD FOR GRADES PRE-K–2
Expectations

In prekindergarten through grade 2 all students should—

- recognize, name, build, draw, compare, and sort two- and three-dimensional shapes;
- describe attributes and parts of two- and three-dimensional shapes;
- investigate and predict the results of putting together and taking apart two- and three-dimensional shapes;
- describe, name, and interpret relative positions in space and apply ideas about relative position; …
- find and name locations with simple relationships such as "near to" and in coordinate systems such as maps;
- recognize and apply slides, flips, and turns;

- recognize and create shapes that have symmetry;
- create mental images of geometric shapes using spatial memory and spatial visualization;
- recognize and represent shapes from different perspectives;
- relate ideas in geometry to ideas in number and measurement;
- recognize geometric shapes and structures in the environment and specify their location.

MEASUREMENT STANDARD FOR GRADES PRE-K–2
Expectations

In prekindergarten through grade 2 all students should—

- recognize the attributes of length, volume, weight, area, and time;
- compare and order objects according to these attributes;
- understand how to measure using nonstandard and standard units;
- select an appropriate unit and tool for the attribute being measured;
- measure with multiple copies of units of the same size, such as paper clips laid end to end; …
- use tools to measure….

DATA ANALYSIS AND PROBABILITY STANDARD FOR GRADES PRE-K–2
Expectations

In prekindergarten through grade 2 all students should—

- pose questions and gather data about themselves and their surroundings;
- sort and classify objects according to their attributes and organize data about the objects;
- represent data using concrete objects, pictures, and graphs;
- describe parts of the data and the set of data as a whole to determine what the data show;
- discuss events related to students' experiences as likely or unlikely.

PROBLEM SOLVING STANDARD FOR GRADES PRE-K–2

Instructional programs from prekindergarten through grade 12 should enable all students to—

- [b]uild new mathematical knowledge through problem solving;
- [s]olve problems that arise in mathematics and in other contexts;
- [a]pply and adapt a variety of appropriate strategies to solve problems;
- [m]onitor and reflect on the process of mathematical problem solving.

REASONING AND PROOF STANDARD FOR GRADES PRE-K–2

Instructional programs from prekindergarten through grade 12 should enable all students to—

- [r]ecognize reasoning and proof as fundamental aspects of mathematics;
- [m]ake and investigate mathematical conjectures;
- [d]evelop and evaluate mathematical arguments and proofs;
- [s]elect and use various types of reasoning and methods of proof.

COMMUNICATION STANDARD FOR GRADES PRE-K–2

Instructional programs from prekindergarten through grade 12 should enable all students to—

- [o]rganize and consolidate their mathematical thinking through communication;
- [c]ommunicate their mathematical thinking coherently and clearly to peers, teachers, and others;
- [a]nalyze and evaluate the mathematical thinking and strategies of others;
- [u]se the language of mathematics to express mathematical ideas precisely.

CONNECTIONS STANDARD FOR GRADES PRE-K–2

Instructional programs from prekindergarten through grade 12 should enable all students to—

- [r]ecognize and use connections among mathematical ideas;
- [u]nderstand how mathematical ideas interconnect and build on one another to produce a coherent whole;
- [r]ecognize and apply mathematics in contexts outside of mathematics.

REPRESENTATION STANDARD FOR GRADES PRE-K–2

Instructional programs from prekindergarten through grade 12 should enable all students to—

- [c]reate and use representations to organize, record, and communicate mathematical ideas;
- [s]elect, apply, and translate among mathematical representations to solve problems;
- [u]se representations to model and interpret physical, social, and mathematical phenomena.

Appendix B

EARLY CHILDHOOD MATHEMATICS: PROMOTING GOOD BEGINNINGS

A joint position statement of the National Association for the Education of Young Children (NAEYC) and the National Council of Teachers of Mathematics (NCTM)

POSITION

The National Council of Teachers of Mathematics (NCTM) and the National Association for the Education of Young Children (NAEYC) affirm that high-quality, challenging, and accessible mathematics education for 3- to 6-year-old children is a vital foundation for future mathematics learning. In every early childhood setting, children should experience effective, research-based curriculum and teaching practices. Such high-quality classroom practice requires policies, organizational supports, and adequate resources that enable teachers to do this challenging and important work.

THE CHALLENGES

Throughout the early years of life, children notice and explore mathematical dimensions of their world. They compare quantities, find patterns, navigate in space, and grapple with real problems such as balancing a tall block building or sharing a bowl of crackers fairly with a playmate. Mathematics helps children make sense of their world outside of school and helps them construct a solid foundation for success in school. In elementary and middle school, children need mathematical understanding and skills not only in math courses but also in science, social studies, and other subjects. In high school, students need mathematical proficiency to succeed in course work that provides a gateway to technological literacy and higher education [1–4]. Once out of school, all adults need a broad range of basic mathematical understanding to make informed decisions in their jobs, households, communities, and civic lives.

Besides ensuring a sound mathematical foundation for all members of our society, the nation also needs to prepare increasing numbers of young people for

work that requires a higher proficiency level [5, 6]. The National Commission on Mathematics and Science Teaching for the 21st Century (known as the Glenn Commission) asks this question: "As our children move toward the day when their decisions will be the ones shaping a new America, will they be equipped with the mathematical and scientific tools needed to meet those challenges and capitalize on those opportunities?" [7, p. 6]

Since the 1970s a series of assessments of U.S. students' performance has revealed an overall level of mathematical proficiency well below what is desired and needed [5, 8, 9]. In recent years NCTM and others have addressed these challenges with new standards and other resources to improve mathematics education, and progress has been made at the elementary and middle school levels—especially in schools that have instituted reforms [e.g., 10–12]. Yet achievement in mathematics and other areas varies widely from state to state [13] and from school district to school district. There are many encouraging indicators of success but also areas of continuing concern. In mathematics as in literacy, children who live in poverty and who are members of linguistic and ethnic minority groups demonstrate significantly lower levels of achievement [14–17].

If progress in improving the mathematics proficiency of Americans is to continue, much greater attention must be given to *early* mathematics experiences. Such increased awareness and effort recently have occurred with respect to early foundations of literacy. Similarly, increased energy, time, and wide-scale commitment to the early years will generate significant progress in mathematics learning.

The opportunity is clear: Millions of young children are in child care or other early education settings where they can have significant early mathematical experiences. Accumulating research on children's capacities and learning in the first six years of life confirms that early experiences have long-lasting outcomes [14, 18]. Although our knowledge is still far from complete, we now have a fuller picture of the mathematics young children are able to acquire and the practices to promote their understanding. This knowledge, however, is not yet in the hands of most early childhood teachers in a form to effectively guide their teaching. It is not surprising then that a great many early childhood programs have a considerable distance to go to achieve high-quality mathematics education for children age 3-6.

In 2000, with the growing evidence that the early years significantly affect mathematics learning and attitudes, NCTM for the first time included the prekindergarten year in its *Principles and Standards for School Mathematics (PSSM)* [19]. Guided by six overarching principles—regarding equity, curriculum, teaching, learning, assessment, and technology—PSSM describes for each mathematics content and process area what children should be able to do from prekindergarten through second grade.

NCTM PRINCIPLES FOR SCHOOL MATHEMATICS

Equity: Excellence in mathematics education requires equally high expectations and strong support for all students.

Curriculum: A curriculum is more than a collection of activities; it must be coherent, focused on important mathematics, and well articulated across the grades.

Teaching: Effective mathematics teaching requires understanding of what students know and need to learn and then challenging and supporting them to learn it well.

Learning: Students must learn mathematics with understanding, actively building new knowledge from experience and prior knowledge.

Assessment: Assessment should support the learning of important mathematics and furnish useful information to both teachers and students.

Technology: Technology is essential to teaching and learning mathematics; it influences the mathematics that is taught and enhances students' learning.

Note: These principles, are relevant across all grade levels, including early childhood.

The present statement focuses on children over 3, in large part because the knowledge base on mathematical learning is more robust for this age group. Available evidence, however, indicates that children under 3 enjoy and benefit from various kinds of mathematical explorations and experiences.

With respect to mathematics education beyond age 6, the recommendations on classroom practice presented here remain relevant. Further, closely connecting curriculum and teaching for children age 3–6 with what is done with students over 6 is essential to achieve the seamless mathematics education that children need.

Recognition of the importance of good beginnings, shared by NCTM and NAEYC, underlies this joint position statement. The statement describes what constitutes high-quality mathematics education for children 3–6 and what is necessary to achieve such quality. To help achieve this goal the position statement sets forth 10 research-based, essential recommendations to guide classroom[1] practice, as well as four recommendations for policies, systems changes, and other actions needed to support these practices.

RECOMMENDATIONS

In high-quality mathematics education for 3- to 6-year-old children, teachers and other key professionals should

1. enhance children's natural interest in mathematics and their disposition to use it to make sense of their physical and social worlds

2. build on children's experience and knowledge, including their family, linguistic, cultural, and community backgrounds; their individual approaches to learning; and their informal knowledge

3. base mathematics curriculum and teaching practices on knowledge of young children's cognitive, linguistic, physical, and social-emotional development

4. use curriculum and teaching practices that strengthen children's problem-solving and reasoning processes as well as representing, communicating, and connecting mathematical ideas

5. ensure that the curriculum is coherent and compatible with known relationships and sequences of important mathematical ideas

6. provide for children's deep and sustained interaction with key mathematical ideas

7. integrate mathematics with other activities and other activities with mathematics

8. provide ample time, materials, and teacher support for children to engage in play, a context in which they explore and manipulate mathematical ideas with keen interest

9. actively introduce mathematical concepts, methods, and language through a range of appropriate experiences and teaching strategies

10. support children's learning by thoughtfully and continually assessing all children's mathematical knowledge, skills, and strategies.

To support high-quality mathematics education, institutions, program developers, and policymakers should

1. create more effective early childhood teacher preparation and continuing professional development

2. use collaborative processes to develop well-aligned systems of appropriate high-quality standards, curriculum, and assessment

3. design institutional structures and policies that support teachers' ongoing learning, teamwork, and planning

4. provide resources necessary to overcome the barriers to young children's mathematical proficiency at the classroom, community, institutional, and system-wide levels.

---

1. *Classroom* refers to any group setting for 3- to 6-year-olds (e.g., child care program, family child care, preschool, or public school classroom).

WITHIN THE CLASSROOM

To achieve high-quality mathematics education for 3- to 6-year-old children, teachers[2] and other key professionals should

1. *Enhance children's natural interest in mathematics and their disposition to use it to make sense of their physical and social worlds.*

Young children show a natural interest in and enjoyment of mathematics. Research evidence indicates that long before entering school children spontaneously explore and use mathematics—at least the intuitive beginnings—and their mathematical knowledge can be quite complex and sophisticated [20]. In play and daily activities, children often explore mathematical ideas and processes; for example, they sort and classify, compare quantities, and notice shapes and patterns [21–27].

Mathematics helps children make sense of the physical and social worlds around them, and children are naturally inclined to use mathematics in this way ("He has more than I do!" "That won't fit in there—it's too big"). By capitalizing on such moments and by carefully planning a variety of experiences with mathematical ideas in mind, teachers cultivate and extend children's mathematical sense and interest.

Because young children's experiences fundamentally shape their attitude toward mathematics, an engaging and encouraging climate for children's early encounters with mathematics is important [19]. It is vital for young children develop confidence in their ability to understand and use mathematics—in other words, to see mathematics as within their reach. In addition, positive experiences with using mathematics to solve problems help children to develop dispositions such as curiosity, imagination, flexibility, inventiveness, and persistence that contribute to their future success in and out of school [28].

2. *Build on children's experience and knowledge, including their family, linguistic, cultural, and community backgrounds; their individual approaches to learning; and their informal knowledge.*

Recognizing and building on children's individual experiences and knowledge are central to effective early childhood mathematics education [e.g., 20, 22, 29, 30]. While striking similarities are evident in the mathematical issues that interest children of different backgrounds [31], it is also true that young children have varying cultural, linguistic, home, and community experiences on which to build mathematics learning [16, 32]. For example, number naming is regular in Asian languages such as Korean (the Korean word for "eleven" is *ship ill*, or "ten one"), while English uses the irregular word *eleven*. This difference appears to make it easier for Korean children to learn or construct certain numerical concepts [33, 34]. To achieve equity and educational effectiveness, teachers must know as much as they can about such differences and work to build bridges between children's varying experiences and new learning [35–37].

In mathematics, as in any knowledge domain, learners benefit from having a variety of ways to understand a given concept [5, 14]. Building on children's individual strengths and learning styles makes mathematics curricu-

---

2. Teachers refers to adults who care for and educate groups of young children.

lum and instruction more effective. For example, some children learn especially well when instructional materials and strategies use geometry to convey number concepts [38].

Children's confidence, competence, and interest in mathematics flourish when new experiences are meaningful and connected with their prior knowledge and experience [19, 39]. At first, young children's understanding of a mathematical concept is only intuitive. Lack of explicit concepts sometimes prevents the child from making full use of prior knowledge and connecting it to school mathematics. Therefore, teachers need to find out what young children already understand and help them begin to understand these things mathematically. From ages 3 through 6, children need many experiences that call on them to relate their knowledge to the vocabulary and conceptual frameworks of mathematics—in other words, to "mathematize" what they intuitively grasp. Toward this end, effective early childhood programs provide many such opportunities for children to represent, reinvent, reorganize, quantify, abstract, generalize, and refine that which they grasp at an experiential or intuitive level [28].

3. Base mathematics curriculum and teaching practices on knowledge of young children's cognitive, linguistic, physical, and social-emotional development.

All decisions regarding mathematics curriculum and teaching practices should be grounded in knowledge of children's development and learning across all interrelated areas—cognitive, linguistic, physical, and social-emotional. First, teachers need broad knowledge of children's cognitive development—concept development, reasoning, and problem solving, for instance—as well as their acquisition of particular mathematical skills and concepts. Although children display mathematical ideas at early ages [e.g., 40–43] their ideas are often very different from those of adults [e.g., 26, 44]. For example, young children tend to believe that a long line of pennies has more coins than a shorter line with the same number.

Beyond cognitive development, teachers need to be familiar with young children's social, emotional, and motor development, all of which are relevant to mathematical development. To determine which puzzles and manipulative materials are helpful to support mathematical learning, for instance, teachers combine their knowledge of children's cognition with the knowledge of fine-motor development [45]. In deciding whether to let a 4-year-old struggle with a particular mathematical problem or to offer a clue, the teacher draws on more than an understanding of the cognitive demands involved. Important too are the teacher's understanding of young children's emotional development and her sensitivity to the individual child's frustration tolerance and persistence [45, 46].

For some mathematical topics, researchers have identified a developmental continuum or learning path—a sequence indicating how particular concepts and skills build on others [44, 47, 48]. Snapshots taken from a few such sequences are given in the accompanying chart.

Research-based generalizations about what *many* children in a given grade or age range can do or understand are key in shaping curriculum and instruction, although they are only a starting point. Even with comparable learning opportunities, some children will grasp a concept earlier and others somewhat later. Expecting and planning for such individual variation are always important.

With the enormous variability in young children's development, neither policymakers nor teachers should set a fixed timeline for children to reach each specific learning objective [49]. In addition to the risk of misclassifying individual children, highly specific timetables for skill acquisition pose another serious threat, especially when accountability pressures are intense. They tend to focus teachers' attention on getting children to perform narrowly defined skills by a specified time, rather than on laying the conceptual groundwork that will serve children well in the long run. Such prescriptions often lead to superficial teaching and rote learning at the expense of real understanding. Under these conditions, children may develop only a shaky foundation for further mathematics learning [50–52].

4. Use curriculum and teaching practices that strengthen children's problem-solving and reasoning processes as well as representing, communicating, and connecting mathematical ideas.

Problem solving and reasoning are the heart of mathematics. Teaching that promotes proficiency in these and other mathematical processes is consistent with national reports on mathematics education [5, 19, 53] and recommendations for early childhood practice [14, 46]. While content represents the *what* of early childhood mathematics education, the processes—problem solving, reasoning, communication, connections, and representation—make it possible for children to acquire content knowledge [19]. These processes develop over time and when supported by well-designed opportunities to learn.

Children's development and use of these processes are among the most long-lasting and important achievements of mathematics education. Experiences and intuitive ideas become truly mathematical as the children reflect on them, represent them in various ways, and connect them to other ideas [19, 47].

The process of making connections deserves special attention. When children connect number to geometry (for example, by counting the sides of shapes, using arrays to understand number combinations, or measuring the length of their classroom), they strengthen concepts from both areas and build knowledge and beliefs about mathematics as a coherent system [19, 47]. Similarly, helping children connect mathematics to other subjects, such as science, develops knowledge of both subjects as well as knowledge of the wide applicability of mathematics. Finally and critically, teaching concepts and skills in a connected, integrated fashion tends to be particularly effective not only in the early childhood years [14, 23] but also in future learning [5, 54].

5. Ensure that the curriculum is coherent and compatible with known relationships and sequences of important mathematical ideas.

In developing early mathematics curriculum, teachers need to be alert to children's experiences, ideas, and creations [55, 56]. To create coherence and power in the curriculum, however, teachers also must stay focused on the "big ideas" of mathematics and on the connections and sequences among those ideas [23, 57].

The big ideas or vital understandings in early childhood mathematics are those that are mathematically central, accessible to children at their present level of understanding, and generative of future learning [28]. Research and expert practice indicate that certain concepts and skills are both challenging and accessible to young children [19]. National professional standards outline core ideas in each of five major content areas: number and operations, geometry, measurement, algebra (including patterns), and data analysis [19]. For example, the idea that the same pattern can describe different situations is a "big idea" within the content area of algebra and patterning.

These content areas and their related big ideas, however, are just a starting point. Where does one begin to build understanding of an idea such as "counting" or "symmetry," and where does one take this understanding over the early years of school? Articulating goals and standards for young children as a developmental or learning continuum is a particularly useful strategy in ensuring engagement with and mastery of important mathematical ideas [49]. In the key areas of mathematics, researchers have at least begun to map out trajectories or paths of learning—that is, the sequence in which young children develop mathematical understanding and skills [21, 58, 59]. The adjacent chart provides brief examples of learning paths in each content area and a few teaching strategies that promote children's progress along these paths. Information about such learning paths can support developmentally appropriate teaching, illuminating various avenues to understanding and guiding teachers in providing activities appropriate for children as individuals and as a group.

6. Provide for children's deep and sustained interaction with key mathematical ideas.

In many early childhood programs, mathematics makes only fleeting, random appearances. Other programs give mathematics adequate time in the curriculum but attempt to cover so many mathematical topics that the result is superficial and uninteresting to children. In a more effective third alternative, children encounter concepts in depth and in a logical sequence. Such depth and coherence allow children to develop, construct, test, and reflect on their mathematical understandings [10, 23, 59, 60]. This alternative also enhances teachers' opportunities to determine gaps in children's understanding and to take time to address these.

Because curriculum depth and coherence are important, unplanned experiences with mathematics are clearly not enough. Effective programs also include intentionally organized learning experiences that build children's understanding over time. Thus, early childhood educators need to plan for children's in-depth involvement with mathematical ideas, including helping families extend and develop these ideas outside of school.

Depth is best achieved when the program focuses on a number of key content areas rather than trying to cover every topic or skill with equal weight. As articulated in professional standards, researchers have identified number and operations, geometry, and measurement as areas particularly important for 3- to 6-year-olds [19]. These play an especially significant role in building the foundation for mathematics learning [47]. For this reason, researchers recommend that algebraic thinking and data analysis/probability receive somewhat less emphasis in the early years. The beginnings of ideas in these two areas, however, should be woven into the curriculum where they fit most naturally and seem most likely to promote understanding of the other topic areas [19]. Within this second tier of content areas, patterning (a component of algebra) merits special mention because it is accessible and interesting to young children, grows to undergird all algebraic thinking, and supports the development of number, spatial sense, and other conceptual areas.

7. *Integrate mathematics with other activities and other activities with mathematics.*

Young children do not perceive their world as if it were divided into separate cubbyholes such as "mathematics" or "literacy" [61]. Likewise, effective practice does not limit mathematics to one specified period or time of day. Rather, early childhood teachers help children develop mathematical knowledge throughout the day and across the curriculum. Children's everyday activities and routines can be used to introduce and develop important mathematical ideas [55, 59, 60, 62–67]. For example, when children are lining up, teachers can build in many opportunities to develop an understanding of mathematics. Children wearing something red can be asked to get in line *first*, those wearing blue to get in line *second*, and so on. Or children wearing both something red *and* sneakers can be asked to head up the line. Such opportunities to build important mathematical vocabulary and concepts abound in any classroom, and the alert teacher takes full advantage of them.

Also important is weaving mathematics into children's experiences with literature, language, science, social studies, art, movement, and music and all parts of the classroom environment. For example, there are books with mathematical concepts in the reading corner, and clipboards and wall charts are placed where children are engaged in science observation and recording (e.g., measuring and charting the weekly growth of plants) [65, 66, 68–71].

Projects also reach across subject-matter boundaries. Extended investigations offer children excellent opportunities to apply mathematics as well as to develop independence, persistence, and flexibility in making sense of real-life problems [19]. When children pursue a project or investigation, they encounter many mathematical problems and questions. With teacher guidance, children think about how to gather and record information and develop representations to help them in understanding and using the information and communicating their work to others [19, 72].

Another rationale for integrating mathematics throughout the day lies in easing competition for time in an increasingly crowded curriculum. Heightened attention to literacy is vital but can make it difficult for teachers to give mathematics and other areas their due. With a strong interdisciplinary curriculum, teachers can still focus on one area at times but also find ways to promote children's competence in literacy, mathematics, and other subjects within integrated learning experiences [73].

An important final note: As valuable as integration is within early childhood curriculum, it is not an end in itself. Teachers should ensure that the mathematics experiences woven throughout the curriculum follow logical sequences, allow depth and focus, and help children move forward in knowledge and skills. The curriculum should not become, in the name of integration, a grab bag of any mathematics-related experiences that seem to relate to a theme or project. Rather, concepts should be developed in a coherent, planful manner.

8. Provide ample time, materials, and teacher support for children to engage in play, a context in which they explore and manipulate mathematical ideas with keen interest.

Children become intensely engaged in play. Pursuing their own purposes, they tend to tackle problems that are challenging enough to be engrossing yet not totally beyond their capacities. Sticking with a problem—puzzling over it and approaching it in various ways—can lead to powerful learning. In addition, when several children grapple with the same problem, they often come up with different approaches, discuss, and learn from one another [74, 75]. These aspects of play tend to prompt and promote thinking and learning in mathematics and in other areas.

Play does not guarantee mathematical development, but it offers rich possibilities. Significant benefits are more likely when teachers follow up by engaging children in reflecting on and representing the mathematical ideas that have emerged in their play. Teachers enhance children's mathematics learning when they ask questions that provoke clarifications, extensions, and development of new understandings [19].

Block building offers one example of play's value for mathematical learning. As children build with blocks, they constantly accumulate experiences with the ways in which objects can be related, and these experiences become the foundation for a multitude of mathematical concepts—far beyond simply sorting and seriating. Classic unit blocks and other construction materials such as connecting blocks give children entry into a world where objects have predictable similarities and relationships [66, 76]. With these materials, children reproduce objects and structures from their daily lives and create abstract designs by manipulating pattern, symmetry, and other elements [77]. Children perceive geometric notions inherent in the blocks (such as two square blocks as the equivalent of one rectangular unit block) and the structures they build with them (such as symmetric buildings with parallel sides). Over time, children can be guided from an intuitive to a more explicit conceptual understanding of these ideas [66].

A similar progression from intuitive to explicit knowledge takes place in other kinds of play. Accordingly, early childhood programs should furnish materials and sustained periods of time that allow children to learn mathematics through playful activities that encourage counting, measuring, constructing with blocks, playing board and card games, and engaging in dramatic play, music, and art [19, 64].

Finally, the teacher can observe play to learn more about children's development and interests and use this knowledge to inform curriculum and instruction. With teacher guidance, an individual child's play interest can develop into a classroom-wide, extended investigation or project that includes rich mathematical learning [78–82]. In classrooms in which teachers are alert to all these possibilities, children's play continually stimulates and enriches mathematical explorations and learning.

9. Actively introduce mathematical concepts, methods, and language through a range of appropriate experiences and teaching strategies.

A central theme of this position statement is that early childhood curriculum needs to go beyond sporadic, hit-or-miss mathematics. In effective programs, teachers make judicious use of a variety of approaches, strategies, and materials to support children's interest and ability in mathematics.

Besides embedding significant mathematics learning in play, classroom routines, and learning experiences across the curriculum, an effective early mathematics program also provides carefully planned experiences that focus children's attention on a particular mathematical idea or set of related ideas. Helping children name such ideas as *horizontal* or *even* and *odd* as they find and create many examples of these categories provides children with a means to connect and refer to their just-emerging ideas [35, 37]. Such concepts can be introduced and explored in large and small group activities and learning centers. Small groups are particularly well suited to focusing children's attention on an idea. Moreover, in this setting the teacher is able to observe what each child does and does not understand and engage each child in the learning experience at his own level.

In planning for new investigations and activities, teachers should think of ways to engage children in revisiting concepts they have previously explored. Such experiences enable children to forge links between previously encountered mathematical ideas and new applications [19].

Even the way that teachers introduce and modify games can promote important mathematical concepts and provide opportunities for children to practice skills [55, 57]. For example, teachers can modify any simple board game in which players move along a path to make the game more mathematically powerful and more appropriate for children of differing developmental levels [55, 83].

Use of materials also requires intentional planning and involvement on the teacher's part. Computer technology is a good example [84]. Teachers need to intentionally select and use research-based computer tools that complement and expand what can be done with other media [59]. As with other instructional materials, choosing software and determining how best to incorporate computer use in the day-to-day curriculum requires thoughtful, informed decisionmaking in order for children's learning experiences to be rich and productive.

In short, mathematics is too important to be left to chance, and yet it must also be connected to children's lives. In making all of these choices, effective early childhood teachers build on children's informal mathematical knowledge and experiences, always taking children's cultural background and language into consideration [23].

10. Support children's learning by thoughtfully and continually assessing all children's mathematical knowledge, skills, and strategies.

Assessment is crucial to effective teaching [87]. Early childhood mathematics assessment is most useful when it aims to help young children by identifying their unique strengths and needs so as to inform teacher planning. Beginning with careful observation, assessment uses multiple sources of information gathered systematically over time—for example, a classroom book documenting the graphs made by children over several weeks. Mathematics assessment should follow widely accepted principles for varied and authentic early childhood assessment [87]. For instance, the teacher needs to use multiple assessment approaches to find out what each child understands—and may misunderstand. Child observation, documentation of children's talk, interviews, collections of children's work over time, and the use of open-ended questions and appropriate performance assessments to illuminate children's thinking are positive approaches to assessing mathematical strengths and needs [88, 89].

Careful assessment is especially important when planning for ethnically, culturally, and linguistically diverse young children and for children with special needs or disabilities. Effective teachers use information and insights gathered from assessment to plan and adapt teaching and curriculum. They recognize that even young children invent their own mathematical ideas and strategies and that children's ideas can be quite different from those of adults [44]. They interpret what the child is doing and thinking, and they attempt to see the situation from the child's point of view. With this basis in thoughtful assessment, teachers are able to make informed decisions about what the child might be able to learn from new experiences.

Reliance on a single group-administered test to document 3- to 6-year-old children's mathematical competence is counter to expert recommendations on assessment of young children [87, 90–93]. Educators must take care that assessment does not narrow the curriculum and inappropriately label children. If assessment results exclude some children from challenging learning activities, they undercut educational equity. Teachers and education policymakers need to stay in control of the assessment process, ensuring that it helps build mathematical competence and confidence. Well-conceived, well-implemented, continuous assessment is an indispensable tool in facilitating all children's engagement and success in mathematics.

BEYOND THE CLASSROOM

To support excellent early mathematics education, institutions, program developers, and policymakers should . . .

1. Create more effective early childhood teacher preparation and continuing professional development.

Improving early childhood teacher preparation and ongoing professional development is an urgent priority. In mathematics, as in literacy and other areas, the challenges are formidable, but research-based solutions are available [14, 94–97]. To support children's mathematical proficiency, every early childhood teacher's professional preparation should include these connected components: (1) knowledge of the mathematical content and concepts most relevant for young children—including in-depth understanding of what children are learning now and how today's learning points toward the horizons of later learning [5]; (2) knowledge of young children's learning and development in all areas—including but not limited to cognitive development—and knowledge of the issues and topics that may engage children at different points in their development; (3) knowledge of effective ways of teaching mathematics to *all* young learners; (4) knowledge and skill in observing and documenting young children's mathematical activities and understanding; and (5) knowledge of resources and tools that promote mathematical competence and enjoyment [98].

Essential as this knowledge is, it can be brought to life only when teachers themselves have positive attitudes about mathematics. Lack of appropriate preparation may cause both preservice and experienced teachers to fail to see mathematics as a priority for young children and to lack confidence in their ability to teach mathematics effectively [99]. Thus, both preservice education and continuing professional development experiences need to place greater emphasis on encouraging teachers' own enjoyment and confidence, building positive mathematical attitudes and dispositions.

Even graduates of four-year early childhood programs with state licensure usually lack adequate preparation in mathematics. State legislatures often address their concern over teachers' weak background in mathematics by simply increasing the number of required mathematics courses needed for teacher licensure. This remedy lacks research support [5, 94]. Credit hours or yearly training requirements do little or nothing unless the content and delivery of professional development are designed to produce desired outcomes for teachers and children [95].

Teachers of young children should learn the mathematics content that is directly relevant to their professional role. But content alone is not enough. Effective professional programs weave together mathematics content, pedagogy, and knowledge of child development and family relationships [100]. When high-quality, well-supervised field work is integrated throughout a training program, early childhood teachers can apply their knowledge in realistic contexts. Courses or inservice training should be designed to help teachers develop a deep understanding of the mathematics they will teach and the habits of mind of a mathematical thinker. Courses, practicum experiences, and other training should strengthen teachers' ability to ask young children the kinds of questions that stimulate mathematical thinking. Effective professional development, whether preservice or inservice, should also model the kind of flexible, interactive teaching styles that work well with children [94].

Preservice and inservice professional development presents somewhat differing challenges. In preservice education, the major challenge is to build a sound, well-integrated knowledge base about mathematics, young children's development and learning, and classroom practices [5]. Inservice training shares this challenge but also carries risks of superficiality and fragmentation.

To avoid these risks, inservice professional development needs to move beyond the one-time workshop to deeper exploration of key mathematical topics as they connect with young children's thinking and with classroom practices. Inservice professional development in mathematics appears to have the greatest impact on teacher learning if it incorporates six features: teacher networking or study groups; sustained, intensive programs; collective participation of staff who work in similar settings; content focused both on what and how to teach; active learning techniques; and professional development as part of a coherent program of teacher learning [5, 102]. Innovative and effective professional development models may use a variety of research-based approaches. In addition, classroom-based inquiry, team teaching by mathematics and early childhood education specialists, discussion of case studies, and analysis of young children's work samples tend to strengthen teachers' confidence and engagement in early childhood mathematics [5, 99, 101, 102].

Delivering this kind of ongoing professional development requires a variety of innovative strategies. For early childhood staff living in isolated communities or lacking knowledgeable trainers, distance learning with local facilitators is a promising option. Literacy initiatives are increasingly using itinerant or school-wide specialists; similarly, mathematics education specialists could offer resources to a number of early childhood programs. Partnerships between higher education institutions and local early childhood programs can help provide this support. Finally, school-district-sponsored professional development activities that include participants from community child care centers, family child care, and Head Start programs along with public school kindergarten/primary teachers would build coherence and continuity for teachers and for children's mathematical experiences.

2. *Use collaborative processes to develop well-aligned systems of appropriate high-quality standards, curriculum, and assessment.*

In mathematics, as in other domains, the task of developing curriculum and related goals and assessments has become the responsibility not only of the classroom teacher but also of other educators and policymakers. State agencies, school districts, and professional organizations are engaged in standards setting, defining desired educational and developmental outcomes for children below kindergarten age [13]. This trend represents an opportunity to improve early childhood mathematics education but also presents a challenge. The opportunity is to develop a coherent, developmentally appropriate, and well-aligned system that offers teachers a framework to guide their work. The challenge, especially at the preschool and kindergarten levels, is to ensure that such a framework does not stifle innovation, put children into inappropriate categories, ignore important individual or cultural differences, or result in narrowed and superficial teaching that fails to give children a solid foundation of understanding [49].

To avoid these risks, state agencies and others must work together to develop more coherent systems of standards, curriculum, instruction, and assessment that support the development of mathematical proficiency. To build coherence between preschool and early elementary mathematics, the processes of setting standards and developing early childhood curriculum and assessment systems must include the full range of stakeholders. Participants should include not only public school teachers and administrators but also personnel from center-based programs and family child care, private and public prekindergarten, and Head Start, as well as others who serve young children and their families. Families too should participate as respected partners. Relevant expertise should be sought from professional associations and other knowledgeable sources.

As in all effective standards-setting efforts, early childhood mathematics standards should be coupled with an emphasis on children's opportunities to learn, not just on expectations for their performance. Standards also should be accompanied by descriptions of what young children might be expected to accomplish along a flexible developmental continuum [49]. Standards for early childhood mathematics should connect meaningfully but not rigidly with curriculum. Assessment also should align with curriculum and with standards, following the principles articulated by national groups concerned with appropriate assessment for young children [90–93].

District- or program-level educators are often responsible for selecting or developing curriculum. Decisionmakers can be guided by the general criteria for curriculum adoption articulated in the position statement jointly adopted by NAEYC and the National Association of Early Childhood Specialists in State Departments of Education [87]. In addition, decisionmakers should insist that any mathematics curriculum considered for adoption has been extensively field tested and evaluated with young children.

3. Design institutional structures and policies that support teachers' ongoing learning, teamwork, and planning.

National reports stress the need for teacher planning and collaboration [5, 7, 103, 104], yet few early childhood programs have the structures and supports to enable these processes to take place regularly. Teachers of young children face particular challenges in planning mathematics activities. Early childhood teachers work in diverse settings, and some of these settings pose additional obstacles to teamwork and collaboration. Many early childhood programs, in or out of public school settings, have little or no time available for teacher planning, either individually or in groups. Team meetings and staff development activities occur infrequently.

The institutional divide between teachers in child care, Head Start, or preschool programs and those in public kindergarten and primary programs limits the communication needed for coherent mathematics curriculum. Without communication opportunities, preschool teachers often do not know what kindergarten programs expect, and early elementary teachers may have little idea of the content or pedagogy used in prekindergarten mathematics education. New strategies and structures, such as joint inservice programs and classroom visits, could support these linkages.

In addition, many programs have limited access to specialists who might help teachers as they try to adopt new approaches to early childhood mathematics. Administrators need to reexamine their allocation of resources and their scheduling practices, keeping in mind the value of investing in teacher planning time.

4. Provide the resources necessary to overcome the barriers to young children's mathematical proficiency at the classroom, community, institutional, and system-wide levels.

A variety of resources, some financial and some less tangible, are needed to support implementation of this position statement's recommendations. Partnerships among the business, philanthropic, and government sectors at the national, state, and local levels will improve teaching and learning in all communities, including those that lack equitable access to mathematics education. Universally available early childhood mathematics education can occur only in the context of a comprehensive, well-financed system of high-quality early education, including child care, Head Start, and prekindergarten programs [105–108]. To support universal mathematical proficiency, access to developmentally and educationally effective programs of early education, supported by adequate resources, should be available to all children.

Improvement of early childhood mathematics education also requires substantial investment in teachers' professional development. The mathematics knowledge gap must be bridged with the best tools, including resources for disseminating models of effective practice, videos showing excellent mathematics pedagogy in real-life settings, computer-based professional development resources, and other materials. In addition, resources are needed to support teachers' involvement in professional conferences, college courses, summer institutes, and visits to model sites.

To support effective teaching and learning, mathematics-rich classrooms require a wide array of materials for young children to explore and manipulate [45, 59, 109]. Equity requires that all programs, not just those serving affluent communities, have these resources.

Finally, resources are needed to support families as partners in developing their young children's mathematical proficiency. The growing national awareness of families' central role in literacy development is a good starting point from which to build awareness of families' equally important role in mathematical development [111, 112]. Public awareness campaigns, distribution of materials in ways similar to the successful Reach Out and Read initiative, computer-linked as well as school-based meetings for families, Family Math Nights, and take-home activities such as mathematics games and manipulative materials tailored to the ages, interests, languages, and cultures of the children—these are only a few examples of the many ways in which resources can support families' engagement in their young children's mathematical learning [113, see also the online "Family Math" materials at www.lhs.berkeley.edu/equals/FMnetwork.htm and other resources at www.nctm.org/corners/family/index.htm].

CONCLUSION

A positive attitude toward mathematics and a strong foundation for mathematics learning begin in early childhood. These good beginnings reflect all the characteristics of good early childhood education: deep understanding of children's development and learning; a strong community of teachers, families, and children; research-based knowledge of early childhood curriculum and teaching practices; continuous assessment in the service of children's learning; and an abiding respect for young children's families, cultures, and communities.

To realize this vision, educators, administrators, policymakers, and families must work together—raising awareness of the importance of mathematics in early education, informing others about sound approaches to mathematical teaching and learning, and developing essential resources to support high-quality, equitable mathematical experiences for all young children.

REFERENCES

1. Haycock, K., & S. Huang. 2001. Are today's high school graduates ready? *Thinking K–16* 5 (1): 3–17.

2. Haycock, K. 2001. Youth at the crossroads: Facing high school and beyond. *Thinking K–16* 5 (1): 1–2.

3. Schoenfeld, A.H. 2002. Making mathematics work for all children: Issues of standards, testing, and equity. *Educational Researcher* 31: 13–25.

4. The Education Trust. 2001. Actions for communities and states. *Thinking K–16* 5 (1): 18–21.

5. Kilpatrick, J., J. Swafford, & B. Findell. 2001. *Adding it up: Helping children learn mathematics.* Washington, DC: National Academy Press.

6. U.S. Department of Labor Bureau of Labor Statistics. 2000. The outlook for college graduates, 1998–2008. In *Getting ready pays off!*, U.S. DOE, October 2000, & BLS, Occupational Employment Projections to 2008, in NAB, Workforce Economics 6 (1).

7. Glenn Commission. 2000. *Before it's too late: A report to the nation from the National Commission on Mathematics and Science Teaching for the 21st Century.* Washington, DC: U.S. Department of Education.

8. Mullis, I.V.S., M.O. Martin, A.E. Beaton, E.J. Gonzalez, D.L. Kelly, & T.A. Smith. 1997. *Mathematics achievement in the primary school years: IEA's Third International Mathematics and Science Study (TIMSS).* Chestnut Hill, MA: Center for the Study of Testing, Evaluation, and Educational Policy, Boston College.

9. Mullis, I.V.S., M.O. Martin, E.J. Gonzalez, K.D. Gregory, R.A. Garden, K.M. O'Connor, S.J. Chrostowski, & T.A. Smith. 2000. *TIMSS 1999 international mathematics report.* Boston: International Study Center, Boston College, Lynch School of Education.

10. Fuson, K.C., W.M. Carroll, & J.V. Drueck. 2000. Achievement results for second and third graders using the standards-based curriculum *Everyday Mathematics. Journal for Research in Mathematics Education* 31: 277–95.

11. Mullis, I.V.S., M.O. Martin, E.J. Gonzalez, K.M. O'Connor, S.J. Chrostowski, K.D. Gregory, R.A. Garden, & T.A. Smith. 2001. *Mathematics benchmarking report: TIMSS 1999—Eighth grade.* Chestnut Hill, MA: International Association for the Evaluation of Educational Achievement.

12. Riordan, J.E., & P.E. Noyce. 2001. The impact of two standards-based mathematics curricula on student achievement in Massachusetts. *Journal for Research in Mathematics Education* 32: 368–98.

13. *Education Week.* 2002. Quality Counts 2002: Building blocks for success: State efforts in early-childhood education. *Education Week* (Special issue) 21 (17).

14. Bowman, B.T., M.S. Donovan, & M.S. Burns, eds. 2001. *Eager to learn: Educating our preschoolers.* Washington, DC: National Academy Press.

15. Denton, K., & J. West. 2002. *Children's reading and mathematics achievement in kindergarten and first grade.* Washington, DC: National Center for Education Statistics.

16. Natriello, G., E.L. McDill, & A.M. Pallas. 1990. *Schooling disadvantaged children: Racing against catastrophe.* New York: Teachers College Press.

17. Starkey, P., & A. Klein. 1992. Economic and cultural influence on early mathematical development. In *New directions in child and family research: Shaping Head Start in the nineties,* eds. F. Lamb-Parker, R. Robinson, S. Sambrano, C. Piotrkowski, J. Hagen, S. Randolph, & A. Baker, 440. Washington, DC: Administration on Children, Youth and Families (DHHS).

18. Shonkoff, J.P., & D.A. Phillips, eds. 2000. *From neurons to neighborhoods: The science of early childhood development.* Washington, DC: National Academy Press.

19. National Council of Teachers of Mathematics. 2000. *Principles and standards for school mathematics.* Reston, VA: Author.

20. Seo, K. H., & H. P. Ginsburg. 2004. What is developmentally appropriate in early childhood mathematics education? Lessons from new research. In *Engaging young children in mathematics: Standards for early childhood mathematics*, eds. D.H. Clements, J. Sarama, & A.-M. DiBiase, 91–105. Mahwah, NJ: Lawrence Erlbaum.

21. Baroody, A.J. 2004. The role of psychological research in the development of early childhood mathematics standards. In *Engaging young children in mathematics: Standards for early childhood mathematics*, eds. D.H. Clements, J. Sarama, & A.-M. DiBiase, 149–72. Mahwah, NJ: Lawrence Erlbaum.

22. Clements, D.H., S. Swaminathan, M.-A. Hannibal, & J. Sarama. 1999. Young children's concepts of shape. *Journal for Research in Mathematics Education* 30: 192–212.

23. Fuson, K.C. 2004. Pre-K to grade 2 goals and standards: Achieving 21st century mastery for all. In *Engaging young children in mathematics: Standards for early childhood mathematics*, eds. D.H. Clements, J. Sarama, & A.-M. DiBiase, 105–48. Mahwah, NJ: Lawrence Erlbaum.

24. Gelman, R. 1994. Constructivism and supporting environments. In *Implicit and explicit knowledge: An educational approach,* ed. D. Tirosh, 55–82. Norwood, NJ: Ablex.

25. Ginsburg, H.P., A. Klein, & P. Starkey. 1998. The development of children's mathematical thinking: Connecting research with practice. In *Handbook of child psychology, Volume 4: Child psychology in practice*, eds. W. Damon, I.E. Sigel, & K.A. Renninger, 401–76. New York: John Wiley & Sons.

26. Piaget, J., and B. Inhelder. 1967. *The child's conception of space.* New York: W.W. Norton.

27. Steffe, L.P. 2004. *PSSM* from a constructivist perspective. In *Engaging young children in mathematics: Standards for early childhood mathematics*, eds. D.H. Clements, J. Sarama, & A.-M. DiBiase, 221–52. Mahwah, NJ: Lawrence Erlbaum.

28. Clements, D.H., & Conference Working Group. 2004. Part one: Major themes and recommendations. In *Engaging young children in mathematics: Standards for early childhood mathematics*, eds. D.H. Clements, J. Sarama, & A.-M. DiBiase, 7–72. Mahwah, NJ: Lawrence Erlbaum.

29. Copple, C.E. 2004. Math curriculum in the early childhood context. In *Engaging young children in mathematics: Standards for early childhood mathematics*, eds. D.H. Clements, J. Sarama, & A.-M. DiBiase, 83–87. Mahwah, NJ: Lawrence Erlbaum.

30. Geary, D.C. 1994. *Children's mathematical development: Research and practical applications*. Washington, DC: American Psychological Association.

31. Ginsburg, H.P., S. Pappas, & K.-H. Seo. 2001. Everyday mathematical knowledge: Asking young children what is developmentally appropriate. In *Psychological perspectives on early childhood education: Reframing dilemmas in research and practice,* ed. S.L. Golbeck, 181–219. Mahwah, NJ: Lawrence Erlbaum.

32. Han, Y., & H.P. Ginsburg. 2001. Chinese and English mathematics language: The relation between linguistic clarity and mathematics performance. *Mathematical Thinking and Learning* 3: 201–20.

33. Miura, I.T., C.C. Kim, C.-M. Chang, & Y. Okamoto. 1988. Effects of language characteristics on children's cognitive representation of number: Cross-national comparisons. *Child Development* 59: 1445–50.

34. Park, M. 2000. Linguistic influence on numerical development. *The Mathematics Educator* 10 (1): 19–24.

35. Berk, L.E., & A. Winsler. 1995. *Scaffolding children's learning: Vygotsky and early childhood education.* Washington, DC: National Association for the Education of Young Children.

36. Heath, S.B. 1983. *Ways with words: Language, life, and work in communities and classrooms.* Cambridge, UK: Cambridge University Press.

37. Vygotsky, L.S. [1934] 1986. *Thought and language.* Cambridge, MA: MIT Press.

38. Razel, M., & B.-S. Eylon. 1990. Development of visual cognition: Transfer effects of the Agam program. *Journal of Applied Developmental Psychology* 11: 459–85.

39. Bredekamp, S., & T. Rosegrant. 1995. *Reaching potentials: Transforming early childhood curriculum and assessment.* Volume 2. Washington, DC: National Association for the Education of Young Children.

40. Clements, D.H. 1999. Geometric and spatial thinking in young children. In *Mathematics in the early years,* ed. J.V. Copley, 66–79. Reston, VA: National Council of Teachers of Mathematics.

41. Starkey, P., & R.G. Cooper Jr. 1980. Perception of numbers by human infants. *Science* 210: 1033–35.

42. Starkey, P., E.S. Spelke, & R. Gelman. 1990. Numerical abstraction by human infants. *Cognition* 36: 97–128.

43. Trafton, P.R., & A. Andrews. 2002. *Little kids—Powerful problem solvers: Math stories from a kindergarten classroom.* Portsmouth, NH: Heinemann.

44. Steffe, L.P., & P. Cobb. 1988. *Construction of arithmetical meanings and strategies.* New York: Springer-Verlag.

45. Bronson, M.B. 1995. *The right stuff for children birth to 8: Selecting play materials to support development.* Washington, DC: National Association for the Education of Young Children.

46. Bredekamp, S., & C. Copple, eds. 1997. *Developmentally appropriate practice in early childhood programs*. Revised ed. Washington, DC: National Association for the Education of Young Children.

47. Clements, D.H., J. Sarama, & A.-M. DiBiase, eds. 2004. In *Engaging young children in mathematics: Standards for early childhood mathematics*. Mahwah, NJ: Lawrence Erlbaum.

48. Gravemeijer, K.P.E. 1999. How emergent models may foster the constitution of formal mathematics. *Mathematical Thinking and Learning* 1: 155–77.

49. Bredekamp, S. 2004. Standards for preschool and kindergarten mathematics education. In *Engaging young children in mathematics: Standards for early childhood mathematics*, eds. D.H. Clements, J. Sarama, & A.-M. DiBiase, 77–82. Mahwah, NJ: Lawrence Erlbaum.

50. Carpenter, T.P., M.L. Franke, V. Jacobs, & E. Fennema. 1998. A longitudinal study of invention and understanding in children's multidigit addition and subtraction. *Journal for Research in Mathematics Education* 29: 3–20.

51. Erlwanger, S.H. 1973. Benny's conception of rules and answers in IPI mathematics. *Journal of Children's Mathematical Behavior* 1 (2): 7–26.

52. Kamii, C.K., & A. Dominick. 1998. The harmful effects of algorithms in grades 1–4. In *The teaching and learning of algorithms in school mathematics*, eds. L.J. Morrow & M.J. Kenney, 130–40. Reston, VA: National Council of Teachers of Mathematics.

53. National Research Council. 1989. *Everybody counts: A report to the nation on the future of mathematics education*. Washington, DC: National Academy Press.

54. Sophian, C. 2004. A prospective developmental perspective on early mathematics instruction. In *Engaging young children in mathematics: Standards for early childhood mathematics*, eds. D.H. Clements, J. Sarama, & A.-M. DiBiase, 253–66. Mahwah, NJ: Lawrence Erlbaum.

55. Kamii, C.K., & L.B. Housman. 1999. *Young children reinvent arithmetic: Implications of Piaget's theory*. 2d ed. New York: Teachers College Press.

56. Steffe, L.P. 1991. *Mathematics curriculum design: A constructivist's perspective*. In International perspectives on transforming early childhood mathematics education, eds. L.P. Steffe & T. Wood, 389–98. Hillsdale, NJ: Lawrence Erlbaum.

57. Griffin, S., R. Case, & A. Capodilupo. 1995. Teaching for understanding: The importance of the central conceptual structures in the elementary mathematics curriculum. In *Teaching for transfer: Fostering generalization in learning*, eds. A. McKeough, J. Lupart, & A. Marini. Mahwah, NJ: Lawrence Erlbaum.

58. Clements, D.H. 2002. Linking research and curriculum development. In *Handbook of international research in mathematics education,* ed. L.D. English, 599–630. Mahwah, NJ: Lawrence Erlbaum.

59. Sarama, J. 2004. Technology in early childhood mathematics: Building Blocks™ as an innovative technology-based curriculum. In *Engaging young children in mathematics: Standards for early childhood mathematics,* eds. D.H. Clements, J. Sarama, & A.-M. DiBiase, 361–75. Mahwah, NJ: Lawrence Erlbaum.

60. Griffin, S. 2004. *Number Worlds*: A research-based mathematics program for young children. In *Engaging young children in mathematics: Standards for early childhood mathematics,* eds. D.H. Clements, J. Sarama, & A.-M. DiBiase, 325–42. Mahwah, NJ: Lawrence Erlbaum.

61. Clements, D.H. 2001. Mathematics in the preschool. *Teaching Children Mathematics* 7: 270–75.

62. Basile, C.G. 1999. The outdoors as a context for mathematics in the early years. In *Mathematics in the early years*, ed. J.V. Copley, 156–61. Reston, VA: National Council of Teachers of Mathematics.

63. Casey, M.B., E. Pezaris, & R.L. Nuttall. 1999. Evidence in support of a model that predicts how biological and environmental factors interact to influence spatial skills. *Developmental Psychology* 35, 1237–47.

64. Hildebrandt, C., & B. Zan. 2002. Using group games to teach mathematics. In *Developing constructivist early childhood curriculum: Practical principles and activities*, ed. R. DeVries, 193–208. New York: Teachers College Press.

65. Hong, H. 1999. *Using storybooks to help young children make sense of mathematics. In Mathematics in the early years,* ed. J.V. Copley, 162–68. Reston, VA: National Council of Teachers of Mathematics.

66. Leeb-Lundberg, K. 1996. The block builder mathematician. In *The block book*, ed. E.S. Hirsh. Washington, DC: National Association for the Education of Young Children.

67. Shane, R. 1999. Making connections: A "number curriculum" for preschoolers. In *Mathematics in the early years,* ed. J.V. Copley, 129–34. Reston, VA: National Council of Teachers of Mathematics.

68. Coates, G.D., & J. Franco. 1999. Movement, mathematics, and learning: Experiences using a family learning model. In *Mathematics in the early years*, ed. J.V. Copley, 169–74. Reston, VA: National Council of Teachers of Mathematics.

69. Copley, J.V. 2000. *The young child and mathematics*. Washington, DC: National Association for the Education of Young Children.

70. Goodway, J.D., M. E. Rudisill, M.L. Hamilton, & M.A. Hart. 1999. Math in motion. In *Mathematics in the early years*, ed. J.V. Copley, 175–81. Reston, VA: National Council of Teachers of Mathematics.

71. Kim, S.L. 1999. *Teaching mathematics through musical activities.* In *Mathematics in the early years*, ed. J.V. Copley, 146–50. Reston, VA: National Council of Teachers of Mathematics.

72. Helm, J.H., S. Beneke, & K. Steinheimer. 1998. *Windows on learning: Documenting young children's work.* New York: Teachers College Press.

73. Balfanz, R. 2001. *Developing and assessing young children's mathematical knowledge.* Washington, DC: National Institute for Early Childhood Professional Development, National Association for the Education of Young Children.

74. Nastasi, B.K., & D.H. Clements. 1991. Research on cooperative learning: Implications for practice. *School Psychology Review* 20: 110–31.

75. Yackel, E., P. Cobb, & T. Wood. 1991. Small group interactions as a source of learning opportunities in second grade mathematics. *Journal for Research in Mathematics Education* 22: 390–408.

76. Pratt, C. 1948. *I learn from children.* New York: Simon and Schuster.

77. Ginsburg, H.P., N. Inoue, & K.-H. Seo. 1999. Young children doing mathematics: Observations of everyday activities. In *Mathematics in the early years*, ed. J.V. Copley, 88–100. Reston, VA: National Council of Teachers of Mathematics.

78. Edwards, C., L. Gandini, & G. Forman. 1993. *The hundred languages of children: The Reggio Emilia approach to early childhood education.* Norwood, NJ: Ablex.

79. Helm, J.H., & L.G. Katz. 2001. *Young investigators: The project approach in the early years.* New York: Teachers College Press.

80. Jones, E., & J. Nimmo. 1994. *Emergent curriculum.* Washington, DC: National Association for the Education of Young Children.

81. Katz, L.G., & S.C. Chard, 2000. *Engaging children's minds: The project approach.* 2d ed. Stamford, CT: Ablex.

82. Malaguzzi, L. 1997. *Shoe and meter.* Reggio Emilia, Italy: Reggio Children.

83. Charlesworth, R. 2000. *Experiences in math for young children.* Albany, NY: Delmar.

84. Clements, D.H. 1999. Young children and technology. In *Dialogue on early childhood science, mathematics, and technology education*, ed. G.D. Nelson, 92–105, Washington, DC: American Association for the Advancement of Science.

85. American Educational Research Association. 2000. *AERA position statement concerning high-stakes testing in preK-12 education.* Washington, DC: Author.

86. National Council of Teachers of Mathematics. 2001. *High-stakes testing.* Reston, VA: Author.

87. National Association for the Education of Young Children & the National Association of Early Childhood Specialists in State Departments of Education. 1991. Guidelines for appropriate curriculum content and assessment in programs serving children ages 3 through 8. *Young Children* 46 (3): 21–38.

88. Chittenden, E. 1991. Authentic assessment, evaluation, and documentation of student performance. In *Expanding student assessment*, ed. V. Perrone, 22–31. Alexandria, VA: Association for Supervision and Curriculum Development.

89. Lindquist, M.M., & J.N. Joyner. 2004. In *Engaging young children in mathematics: Standards for early childhood mathematics*, eds. D.H. Clements, J. Sarama, & A.-M. DiBiase, 449–55. Mahwah, NJ: Lawrence Erlbaum.

90. Horm-Wingerd, D.M., P.C. Winter, & P. Plofchan. 2000. *Primary level assessment for IASA Title I: A call for discussion.* Washington, DC: Council of Chief State School Officers.

91. National Association of School Psychologists. 1999. *Position statement on early childhood assessment.* Washington, DC: Author.

92. National Education Goals Panel. 1998. *Principles and recommendations for early childhood assessments* (submitted to NEGP by the Goal 1 Early Childhood Assessments Resource Group, eds. L. Shepard, S.L. Kagan, & E. Wurtz). Washington, DC: U.S. Government Printing Office.

93. Neisworth, J.T., & S.J. Bagnato. 2001. Recommended practices in assessment. In *DEC recommended practices in early intervention/ early childhood special education*, eds. S. Sandall, M.E. McLean, & B.J. Smith, 17–28. Longmont, CO: Sopris West.

94. Conference Board of the Mathematical Sciences. 2001. *The mathematical education of teachers, part one.* Providence, RI: Mathematical Association of America.

95. National Association for the Education of Young Children. 2001. *NAEYC standards for early childhood professional preparation.* Washington, DC: Author.

96. Peisner-Feinberg, E.S., R. Clifford, M. Culkin, C. Howes, & S.L. Kagan. 1999. *The children of the Cost, Quality, and Outcomes Study go to school.* Chapel Hill: Frank Porter Graham Child Development Center, University of North Carolina at Chapel Hill.

97. U.S. Department of Education. 1999. *New teachers for a new century: The future of early childhood professional preparation.* Washington, DC: Author.

98. Copley, J.V., & Y. Padròn. 1999. Preparing teachers of young learners: Professional development of early childhood teachers in mathematics and science. In *Dialogue on early childhood science, mathematics, and technology education*, ed. G.D. Nelson, 117–29. Washington, DC: American Association for the Advancement of Science.

99. Sarama, J., & A.-M. DiBiase. 2004. The professional development challenge in preschool mathematics. In *Engaging young children in mathematics: Standards for early childhood mathematics*, eds. D.H. Clements, J. Sarama, & A.-M. DiBiase, 415–46. Mahwah, NJ: Lawrence Erlbaum.

100. Baroody, A.J., & R.T. Coslick. 1998. *Fostering children's mathematical power: An investigative approach to K–8 mathematics instruction.* Mahwah, NJ: Lawrence Erlbaum.

101. Ball, D., & D. Cohen. 1999. Developing practice, developing practitioners: Toward a practice-based theory of professional education. In *Teaching as the learning profession*, eds. L. Darling-Hammond and L. Sykes. San Francisco: Jossey-Bass.

102. Copley, J.V. 2004 The early childhood collaborative: A professional development model to communicate and implement the standards. In *Engaging young children in mathematics: Standards for early childhood mathematics*, eds. D.H. Clements, J. Sarama, & A.-M. DiBiase, 401–14. Mahwah, NJ: Lawrence Erlbaum.

103. Bransford, J.D., A.L. Brown, & R.R. Cocking, eds. 1999. *How people learn*. Washington, DC: National Academy Press.

104. Darling-Hammond, L. 1990. Instructional policy into practice: "The power of the bottom over the top." *Educational Evaluation and Policy Analysis* 12 (3): 339–47.

105. Barnett, W.S., & L. Masse. 2001. Financing early care and education in the United States: CEER policy brief. New Brunswick, NJ: Center for Early Education Research.

106. *Brandon, R.N., S.L. Kagan, & J.M. Joesch. 2000. Design choices: Universal financing for early care and education.* Seattle: University of Washington.

107. Mitchell, A., L. Stoney, & H. Dichter. 2001. *Financing child care in the United States: An expanded catalog of current strategies.* 2d ed. Kansas City, MO: Ewing Marion Kauffman Foundation.

108. Office of Economic Cooperation and Development. 2000. *OECD country note: Early childhood education and care policy in the United States of America.* Washington, DC: Office for Educational Research and Improvement.

109. Clements, D.H. 2003. Teaching and learning geometry. In *A research companion to Principles and Standards for School Mathematics*, eds. J. Kilpatrick, W.G. Martin, & D.E. Schifter. Reston, VA: National Council of Teachers of Mathematics.

110. Sarama, J. 2000. Toward more powerful computer environments: Developing mathematics software on research-based principles. *Focus on Learning Problems in Mathematics* 22 (3&4): 125–47.

111. Moll, L.C., C. Armanti, D. Neff, & N. Gonzalez. 1992. Funds of knowledge for teaching: Using a qualitative approach to connect homes and classrooms. *Theory into Practice* 31: 132–41.

112. Starkey, P., & A. Klein. 2000. Fostering parental support for children's mathematical development: An intervention with Head Start families. *Early Education and Development* 11: 659–80.

113. Edge, D. 2000. *Involving families in school mathematics: Readings from Teaching Children Mathematics, Mathematics Teaching in the Middle School, and Arithmetic Teacher*. Reston, VA: National Council of Teachers of Mathematics.

Appendix C
Templates for Animal Stick Puppets

HANNY THE HONEY BEAR

YIPPY THE PRAIRE DOG

BABY ELEPHANT

One each for Binky, Boo, Bobo, Baba, Beany, and Bart

LULU THE LLAMA

MORTY THE LONG-LEGGED MOOSE

Appendix D
Templates for Creature Cards

References

Baroody, Arthur J., and Jesse L. M. Wilkins. "The Development of Informal Counting, Number, and Arithmetic Skills and Concepts." In *Mathematics in the Early Years*, edited by Juanita V. Copley, pp. 48–65. Reston, Va.: National Council of Teachers of Mathematics, 1999.

Blaut, James M., and David Stea. "Mapping at the Age of Three." *Journal of Geography* 73 (October 1974): 5–9.

Boynton, Saundra. *Hippos Go Berserk!* New York: Simon & Schuster, 1996.

Brisson, Pat. *Benny's Pennies*. Glenview, Ill.: Scott, Foresman & Co., 1995.

Carle, Eric. *The Secret Birthday Message*. New York: HarperCollins, 1991.

Capucilli, Alyssa Satin. *Mrs. McTats and Her Houseful of Cats*. New York: Margaret K. McElderry Books, 2001.

Casey, Beth, Carol L. Anderson, and Michael Schiro. *Layla Discovers Secret Patterns*. Chicago, Ill.: Wright Group McGraw-Hill, 2002.

Casey, Beth, Anne Goodrow, Michael Schiro, and Karen L. Anderson. *Teeny Visits Shapeland*. Chicago, Ill.: Wright Group McGraw-Hill, 2002.

Casey, Beth, Patricia Paugh, and Nancer Ballard. *Sneeze Builds a Castle*. Chicago, Ill.: Wright Group/McGraw-Hill, 2002.

Clements, Douglas. "Geometric and Spatial Thinking in Young Children." In *Mathematics in the Early Years*, edited by Juanita V. Copley, pp. 66–79. Reston, Va.: National Council of Teachers of Mathematics, 1999.

———. "Geometric and Spatial Thinking in Early Childhood Education." In *Engaging Young Children in Mathematics: Findings of the 2000 National Conference on Standards for Preschool and Kindergarten Mathematics Education,* edited by Douglas. H. Clements, Julie Sarama, and Ann-Marie Dibiase. Mahwah, N.J.: Lawrence Erlbaum Associates, 2003.

Clements, Douglas, and Julie Sarama. DLM Express Math Resource Package. Columbus, Ohio: SRA/McGraw-Hill, 2003.

Clements, Douglas H., Sudha Swaminathan, Mary Anne Zeitler Hannibal, and Julie Sarama. "Young Children's Concepts of Shape." *Journal for Research in Mathematics Education* 30 (March 1999): 192–212.

Copley, Juanita V. *The Young Child and Mathematics*. Washington, D.C.: National Association for the Education of Young Children, 2000.

Copley, Juanita V., ed. *Mathematics in the Early Years*. Reston, Va.: National Council of Teachers of Mathematics, 1999.

Curtis, Jamie Lee. *When I Was Little: A Four-Year-Old's Memoir of Her Youth*. New York: Scholastic, 1993.

Friel, Susan, Frances R. Curcio, and George W. Bright. "Making Sense of Graphs: Critical Factors Influencing Comprehension and Instructional Implications." *Journal for Research in Mathematics Education* 32 (March 2001): 124–58.

Ginsburg, Herbert P., Carole Greenes, and Robert Balfanz. *Big Math for Little Kids*. Dale Seymour Publications, 2003.

Ginsburg, Herbert P., Alice Klein, and Prentice Starkey. "The Development of Children's Mathematical Thinking: Connecting Research with Practice." In *Handbook of Child Psychology, 5th ed., vol. 4, Child Psychology in Practice,* edited by Irving E. Sigel and K. Ann Renninger, pp. 401–76. New York: John Wiley & Sons, 1998.

Graves, Michelle. *100 Small-Group Experiences: The Teacher's Idea Book #3*. Ypsilanti, Mich.: High/Scope Press, 1997.

Jenkins, Emily. *Five Creatures*. New York: Farrar, Strauss and Giroux, 2001.

Kilpatrick, Jeremy, Jane Swafford, and Bradford Findell, eds. *Adding It Up: Helping Children Learn Mathematics*. Washington, D.C.: National Academy Press, 2001.

McBrantley, Sam. *Guess how Much I Love You*. Cambridge, Mass.: Candlewick Press, 1994.

Miller, Margaret. *Now I Am Big*. New York: Greenwillow Books, 1996.

Mosel, Arlene. *Tikki Tikki Tembo*. New York: H. Holt & Co., 1989.

Murphy, Stuart J. *A Pair of Socks*. New York: HarperCollins Publishers, 1996.National Council of Teachers of Mathematics (NCTM). *Principles and Standards for School Mathematics*. Reston, Va.: NCTM, 2000.

National Council of Teachers of Mathematics (NCTM). *Principles and Standards for School Mathematics*. Reston, Va.: NCTM 2000.

Piaget, Jean, and Barbel Inhelder. *The Child's Conception of Space*. New York: W.W. Norton & Co., 1967.

Russell, Susan. Jo. "Counting Noses and Scary Things: Children Construct Their Ideas about Data. In *Proceedings of the Third International Conference on Teaching Statistics,* edited by D. Vere-Jones. Voorburg, Netherlands: International Statistical Institute, 1991.

Shonkoff, Jack P., and Deborah Phillips, eds. *From Neurons to Neighborhoods: The Science of Early Childhood Development*. Washington, D.C.: National Academy Press, 2000.

Siegel, Alexander W., and Margaret Schadler. "The Development of Young Children's Spatial Representations of Their Classrooms." *Child Development* 48 (June 1977): 388–94.

Sierra, Judy. *Counting Crocodiles*. Orlando, Fla.: Harcourt Brace & Co., 1997.

Sophian, Catherine. "A Developmental Perspective on Children's Counting." In *The Development of Mathematical Skills*, edited by Chris Donlan, pp. 27–46. Hove, East Sussex, England: Psychology Press, 1999.

Starkey, Prentice. "Informal Addition." In *The Development of Arithmetic Concepts and Skills: Constructing Adaptive Expertise*, edited by Arthur Baroody and Ann Dowker. Mahwah, N.J.: Lawrence Erlbaum Associates, 2003.

Starkey, Prentice, and Alice Klein. *Pre-K Mathematics Curriculum*. Glenview, Ill.: Scott Foresman, 2002.

Starkey, Prentice, Elizabeth S. Spelke, and Rochel Gelman. "Numerical Abstraction by Human Infants." *Cognition* 36 (August 1990): 97–128.

Uttal, David H., and Henry M. Wellman. "Young Children's Representation of Spatial Information Acquired from Maps." *Developmental Psychology* 25 (January 1989): 128–38.

Wynn, Karen. "Numerical Competence in Infants." In *The Development of Mathematical Skills*, edited by Chris Donlan, pp. 3–26. Hove, East Sussex, England: Psychology Press, 1999.